Steve Jacobsen

Hearts to God
Hands to Work

Connecting Spirituality and Work

An Alban Institute Publication

Library of Congress Catalog Number 96-80119
ISBN 1–56699–180-3

CONTENTS

Searching for the Real World

Which is the real world? The world of banks, mortgages, pension funds, time clocks, credit cards, taxes, and computers? Or the world of prayer, ancient scriptures, clerical vestments, the Eucharist, small group studies, theological position papers, and hymns? The question has been a dominant issue in my life journey.

I grew up in a family dominated by the world of business. My father had returned from the Second World War and begun a career in real estate. Because the fifties and sixties were times of great growth in housing in California, his work was demanding but productive. I remember hearing at the dinner table (hearing, but not understanding) words like "escrow," "appraisal," and "title company." These were words of power and value. Our standard of living rose, and we lived with the expectation that we would enjoy constantly increasing prosperity.

As I grew up, I assumed I too would move into this world, a world that would be the source of my security and meaning. I went to college and studied European history. During these years I had no use for religious institutions or spiritual reality. In the summers, I worked as a messenger for a savings and loan company, as an intern for the California Department of Real Estate, and helping a painting contractor refurbish apartments. In these positions, I worked alongside people making a living; we filled out time cards, shared coffee breaks and lunches, and hoped for Christmas bonuses. I enjoyed the camaraderie of the workplace, the paychecks, and the sense that I was participating in the Real World. I was confident that I would achieve the American dream of prosperity and security by working in the world of commerce and civic affairs.

Toward the end of my undergraduate days, caught up in the lifestyle of the sixties, I made some choices that were not good for my emotional health. On a Sunday night in September 1973, I found myself alone and in a personal crisis, full of anxiety and fear. I was feeling my grip on life slip away. Although I had been a self-professing atheist, I recited the Lord's Prayer with little hope but great need.

Two days later I was at work and realized I had a deep sense of peace. I began searching for a reason for this peace, and suddenly I remembered the trauma I had experienced and the prayer I had said. Stronger than my devout skepticism was a tangible, unmistakable sign that there was another reality "out there," invisible, un-nameable, and silent, but one that could touch me and heal me in a way that ordinary reality could not. While this was to be the foundational experience for my life, at the time I did not believe it had anything to say about my vocation or values.

After graduation, I continued on my career path, working for a title insurance company in Orange County and then as a real estate sales associate in Sacramento. In 1976 I entered law school. Reading the expensive case books and discussing principles of common law and procedure, I felt I was at the center of reality. But quite unexpectedly, that other dimension, that spiritual dimension, began to take on new power. Ann, a woman I had been dating for a year, had decided faith was becoming more important for her and that because it was not important for me, our relationship should end. Resisting what seemed like a trivial reason to end a relationship, I began attending her church as a way to demonstrate I was broad-minded. There, due to some particularly creative preaching and the simple caring of an adult small group, I began to realize that what was going on in this church was related to that silent gift of peace that had saved my life several years before. I heard language I didn't understand—words like "grace," "deacons," and "communion meditation"—and picking up a Bible seemed to me much more intimidating than opening up the real estate code or a text book on criminal procedure. But somehow this spiritual reality, while quite intangible, began to seem more potent. I decided to complete my first year of law school and take a leave of absence to sort all this out.

I left law school, and Ann and I were married. I worked a variety of jobs as we decided what to do. In that year I began to experience the nurturing power of a Christian community. I decided to enroll in seminary in order to try to understand this new reality that seemed to me to be changing my life. We left California and moved to Princeton Seminary in New Jersey.

Seminary was the place where I began to learn the culture of mainline Protestantism. Eventually I became fluent in churchspeak, using words like "grace," "redemption," "sanctification," and "apocalyptic" as if they had always been in my vocabulary. The view I absorbed was that my task was to persuade people to adopt a worldview that was based in Scripture and interpreted conclusively by the great theologians. That view would be coherent for everyone. "Come into this world of faith," my invitation would begin. "Things are clear and orderly here. Everything will make sense. There are answers to life's questions, and I can show you where to find them. The answers are in these books." From the vantage point of seminary, my job was going to be fairly easy.

Following graduation, we returned to southern California, where I worked as an associate pastor for four years. We then moved to rural Washington State to spend a year as volunteers in mission at a farm and retreat center. When our year was up, I began a six-year pastorate in a nearby church.

During these eleven years of ministry, I experienced many blessings in my work. Good and pleasant things were happening in my churches. There were no shortage of precious and profound encounters with people. But I gradually lost some of my illusions about what my work would be like and what I would accomplish. It just didn't seem to be the case that the coherent world of theology that was so self-evidently true to me was as meaningful to the people I worked with. There wasn't any room in my model for some of the ambiguities of life, the stresses of work, the profound sense that in day-to-day life God was not as powerful as other forces. I could be a prophet and point out all the ways the secular world was falling short of the glory and justice of God. But that didn't seem to change anything. (I remember one colleague who had been told by her elderly parishioner: "I come to worship and they tell me to go out and change the world—but it's a big deal for me if I can just make it up the steps.") I could focus on the aspects of my church's institutional life that I understood and that played by theological rules. In this vein, I could train people for working in church leadership roles, form committees and task forces, and advocate the works of outreach and care we were engaged in. I felt good if I could do these tasks well, and people often were grateful. But still I felt as if I were living in a safe lagoon far removed from the turbulent seas that formed the great staging area for most peoples' lives. My denomination had a strong historical tradition of being "in the world," affirming the importance of public life and unafraid of secular realities. But my denomination was in decline. Much of its energy was being spent on responding to factional conflicts and dwindling resources. Bold position papers and statements on social issues had little effect. The "heart" work of Sunday morning worship was not connecting with the work done by people's hands on Mondays. *It was clear to me that I simply was not connecting to people's everyday lives.*

Questions began to arise. Some of these questions arose within me and some from the literature describing the declining influence of mainline religious institutions. Where is the "real world"? Is it within church property and programs? Or is the real world outside? Is the church truly speaking to people's deepest needs, or is it just a civic institution with a limited role, something like a rest stop off a busy interstate? If the predictions come true and mainline churches become extinct in the early part of the next century, what will become of the human search for transcendence?

As I reached midlife, these questions became more ominous. The earlier world I had known—the world of commerce and tangible accomplishment—gradually began to appear more and more compelling to me, while the world of "spiritual" endeavor was losing its luster. I had three children by this point, and I knew that having a job—tangible work—was a nonnegotiable responsibility. I began to explore other career options, ones that might take me back to that world I had known before ordained ministry.

In this time of searching, I found myself assuming I needed to reject one world—the "spiritual" world of church life and ministry—for the other world, the "real" world of secular life and work. But in a book on the spiritual dimension of midlife experience, the authors warned against any temptation to reject parts of ourself and our past. This, they said, can be unnecessarily destructive. An alternative is to try to reconcile and unify competing aspects to produce a richer whole rather than fragmented parts. I found myself wanting to integrate these parts of myself both internally, through continued reflection, and externally, by looking for outward expressions of this kind of integration.

This search led me in 1991 to begin a doctoral program in Seattle.

The program was designed for people who work, and the focus was education with an emphasis on organizational development. Exactly why I was there wasn't completely clear to me, but it felt like the place I needed to be.

While an initial impetus for entering this program had been a possible reentry into secular work, I soon recognized that the search for integration of secular life and spirituality was a common theme among classmates and faculty. Also, as I began to study contemporary works on leadership, business, and organizational development, I was quite surprised to discover that this hunger for integration was affecting the mainstream secular discussion. It became clear to me that the restlessness I was feeling was not mine alone; it was part of a much larger hunger in our society for a way to integrate our working lives with spiritual truth. Many people were exploring how to connect their spiritual hearts and their laboring hands.

When the time came for me to begin my dissertation, I decided to design a research project to explore the importance of spirituality for people who served as effective leaders in secular organizations. The heart of the project was to identify a group of highly esteemed leaders in secular organizations and then to ask them a series of seven questions regarding what role, if any, spirituality played in their life. The project was designed so that I would summarize responses to the questions and circulate these summaries among the participants to see if any consensus was possible.

I was not prepared for the prominence and diversity of people who became involved. People who agreed to identify the leaders who would be surveyed included the former president of the University of California, the president emeritus of Notre Dame, a former ambassador to NATO, and a leading consultant in the Pacific Northwest. Among the twenty-two women and men who were nominated by this panel and who agreed to participate in the study itself were an acting state governor, a United States senator, a Cadillac dealer, a health care administrator, a Xerox executive, the head of a nursing department in a county hospital, several heads of state government departments, and several directors of nonprofit foundations. (For a listing of the panelists and participants, see appendix B.)

In the midst of my research, I received a call from a church back in California. The church was supportive of my finishing my doctoral work.

I discerned a clear sense of leading to accept the call. In the summer of 1992, we moved to Santa Barbara to begin this new position.

In the fall of that year, the first responses in my project were ready for analysis. Before I sat down to review the material, I taped together all the responses to each question to form seven long columns. Reading the responses for the first time gave me a sense of awe. I felt like an archeologist who had just discovered a sacred treasure, or a scientist making a new discovery. Here was a collective testimony to the importance of integrating the spiritual dimension of life with the secular world of work, commerce, and government. No participant claimed such integration was easy, but all described how important the drive for integration was. For them, it was not a case of two separate competing worlds but one reality with different dimensions. Hearts and hands were connected. As this sunk in, I was aware that the wound within me was being healed. Reading the leaders' responses was a turning point in my life, a turn toward integration. (For a listing of the seven consensus statements produced by the study, see appendix C.)

While I worked on completing the study, I found myself beginning to examine some of the working assumptions I held as a clergyperson:

- I began to be aware that my habits of mind led me to perpetuate a sense that the world of God and the world of work are unrelated.
- I became aware of how rarely my sermons referred to the world of work and how little my teaching ministry touched on these concerns.
- I began to realize how often the issues people struggle with involve in some way jobs, money, and vocation.
- As I reflected on my own children and the youth at my church, I realized we were doing nothing to equip them for the soul-work necessary for integrating faith and work.

Over the next two years, I tried to keep track of the implications of my research as I went about the tasks of ministry. I also noticed that books on vocational guidance, work effectiveness, and leadership being published in the secular literature were discussing the importance of spirituality. Some of this material was very helpful, but much of it was written largely without the benefit of the accumulated experience of spiritual traditions. I kept wanting to see the underlying truths in it all, the reality God wants us to see. What follows is what I am learning, both as a pastor and as a human being.

Chapter 1 offers a brief history of how spirituality and work are related, starting with Scripture and moving to the present. The second chapter is an attempt to provide a basic practical theology that takes the role of work into account. The next four chapters offer some suggestions for incorporating issues of work into preaching, pastoral care and spiritual direction, education, and leadership. The final chapter is a closing reflection.

My hope is that this book will be of practical help for anyone who is trying to connect heart work with hand work—to integrate life lived "in the Spirit" and "in the world."

CHAPTER 1

A Brief History of Spirituality and Work

A Yearning for Integration

The tension I have experienced in trying to reconcile the world of work and commerce with the world of spirituality is a tension known to many. Evidence of this conflict is easy to find. Ask people how they relate their faith and their work and notice how often it is difficult for people to respond. One businessman in my church, who has an unusually strong background in biblical knowledge, told me once that he had done a careful study of what Scripture has to say about business and was disappointed that he could find only a few direct references, mostly in the book of Proverbs. Many people spend forty to sixty hours a week working. Why is it so difficult to find any connection between faith and work? To answer this question, it's helpful to understand the way this issue has been understood over the last 3,000 years.

Spirituality and Work in Scripture

The overall panorama of Scripture presents work as a natural part of human life. Consider the role of work in the lives of the following figures:

• Adam is the first human figure to appear, and before anything else is said about him, we hear he has work to do: "The LORD God took the man and put him in the garden of Eden to till it and keep it" (Gen. 2:15).
• Abraham and Sarah are wealthy ranchers who respond to a late-in-life spiritual experience; they must leave the security of their retirement and

take all their possessions with them on the road (12:1-9).

• Two generations later, their great-grandson Joseph achieves power and influence not simply because of some spiritual knowledge but because of his ability to apply that knowledge effectively as a high ranking civil servant in Pharaoh's court. It is in the context of his "job" that God's purposes are played out (39:1-6).

• Moses' spiritual journey takes him through a variety of vocations. As a young man, he does not need to work because he has been taken into the royal household by Pharaoh's daughter, but then he loses that luxury when he kills an Egyptian (Exod. 2:10-15a). As a fugitive in Midian, he gets work as a shepherd through his father-in-law (vv. 15b-21). He finds the burning bush not when he is in a temple but at work (3:1-6).

• David himself is first known as someone who works in the family business as a shepherd (1 Sam. 16:10-13). While he soon proves his worth as a military and political leader, his greatest composition, the Twenty-Third Psalm, uses imagery drawn from his earlier vocation.

While the primary focus of these stories is the relationship between the biblical character and God, the work these people do clearly influences them. The world of Spirit and the world of work are part of one world, known by one God.

When we turn to the New Testament, we find similar themes:

• Following the vocational custom of his time, Jesus works as a carpenter before beginning his ministry (Mark 6:3).

• Peter, Andrew, James, and John work as fishermen (Mark 1:16-20). At some points in the gospels, this fishing work is something they leave behind to pursue their spiritual journeys. But at other times, Jesus teaches them important lessons through the medium of their work. In Luke 5:1-11, for instance, Jesus gives Peter instructions about where to cast his nets, which leads to both a great catch of fish and tangible evidence that this Jesus has powerful knowledge of the "real world." In the resurrection appearance in John 21, spiritual lessons are again learned in the midst of work.

• Matthew is a tax collector. This profession is seen as profoundly "unspiritual" in the culture of the time. But Jesus does not recognize these boundaries and calls Matthew into fellowship (Matt. 9:9).

• Paul is quite intentional about keeping his occupation as a leather worker/tentmaker (Acts 18:1-3). This is a job skill that not only allows him to support himself as he travels but also to preach without fear of economic consequences.

• Lydia becomes a key figure in Paul's work. She is known as a business-woman who has enjoyed commercial success in textiles and is willing to use her resources to further the needs of the community (Acts 16:14).

Clearly, the *primary* theme of the New Testament is the relationship between people and God as mediated by Jesus Christ. But, as in the Hebrew Scriptures, we see the realities of work and vocation are a part of this broad story, not separate from it. Sometimes people must leave secular vocations to pursue deeper relationships with God. At other times their vocations become important parts of their lives, through which God speaks to them and by which they are able to embody their faith. The biblical view sees life not as fragmented but as a whole.

From the First Century to the Twenty-First

A worldview in which the spiritual life and working life are part of one larger whole did not stay intact for long. As the Christian church developed and grew, the world of everyday work became less significant. In the monastic model, the greatest calling for a human being was to separate oneself from the ordinary world for the "inner life" of prayer and contemplation. To be sure, some major figures such as St. Benedict held up the importance of manual labor as a means of discipline and devotion. But a sense of hierarchy emerged in which the average working person— peasant or tradesperson—was seen as intrinsically less holy than a monk, nun, or priest. The greater reality, it was believed, was above and beyond the visible world.

The Reformation counteracted some of this imbalance. John Calvin, for instance, based his work in the commercial center of Geneva and advocated seeing all of life as an appropriate arena for God's purposes. The Reformation doctrine of the "priesthood of all believers" supported the idea that a faithful merchant could be as holy a person as a member of the clergy. While much emphasis remained on the promise of life after death, the ordinary life regained some of its importance. (In the famous work of the sociologist Max Weber, of course, this dramatic shift in worldview brought on by Calvinism became the moving force behind capitalism).

While the Reformation was in many ways a radical departure from Catholicism, both groups shared a view that the world was comprehensible. The discipline that enabled one to see the world as a whole was theology. But this view was not to last.

With the onset of the Enlightenment, the world of reason and science began to take on new life and power. An increasingly popular view of God, particularly among intellectuals, was deism. Deism held that God might have created the physical world, giving it natural law, but from that point onward the world has been on its own. The view that a living God is still active in the world of creation became less credible. Darwinism, of course, was one of the most dramatic disruptions in the old view. Life might or might not have begun with divine purpose, but it effectively continues through trial and error. To understand life, one must turn away from the superstitions of faith and towards the impersonal forces of nature, which can be known through the scientific method.

This trust in rationalism found expression in industrialism, which transformed the life of the West. The realities of the working life were understood to be formed almost entirely by impersonal forces. One great proponent of this view was Frederick Taylor, long thought to be the father of modern management. Taylor sought to apply the scientific method to the workplace. He developed precise procedures to determine the most efficient way to produce a good. Thinking about work was the job of management; the worker was simply the means for accomplishing a task. Heart knowledge was irrelevant. Though Taylor became known as the "enemy of the working man,"[1] his influence on modern industrial life has been enormous. For Taylor, "spirituality" had nothing to do with work. This assumption has dominated organizational theory for decades.

While this change in thinking was going on, the institutions that sought to preserve spiritual traditions were faced with a great challenge. What did they have to say to people who labored as garment workers, bankers, teachers, industrialists, clerks, plyers of trades, and telephone operators? Did a pastor or priest have a liberating and empowering word for the people who were spending five and six days a week in the impersonal world of commerce and industrial power?

One option was to respond to the pain and injustice brought about by industrialism through advocacy and programs. Catholic social teaching often advocated a more compassionate social order. Protestant movements such as the Social Gospel sought to counteract the ravages of economic inequities through political change and relief. Many denominations tried to challenge what was happening. But in general, these efforts had limited impact on the ways of thinking that were driving the industrial society. The industrial and commercial forces had a logic and mind of their own, and the church was largely seen as an outsider.

Another option was for the church to withdraw from any aspiration to speak to the larger questions. The church was a place of moral training, ethical reflection, and charity. But these purposes did not for the most part extend beyond the church itself. The weekday world—the "outer world," the world of commerce—was the "real world." The world of faith—the Sunday morning world, the interior world, the world of theology and spirituality—had its place, but there were clear boundaries limiting its usefulness and influence.

By the 1950s, the major denominations, both Protestant and Catholic, still had some influence over society. By the sixties, however, things began to come apart. Denominational loyalty was dissolving. Membership in mainline churches began a steady decline. Secular society had a momentum of its own, and it was not waiting for the blessing or instruction of the historical religious institutions. Like a geological fault that grows from crack to chasm, the gap between religion and secular reality became profound. But much of theology and practice was slow to accept this change or to address it in any effective manner.

William Diehl has offered a vivid description of what it is like to be a working layperson caught in this gap. In his book *The Monday Connection*, Diehl tells his story as a businessperson becoming involved in a church. Gradually, he began to sense the gap between his Sunday morning community and work on Monday morning. He noticed, for instance, that whenever business was discussed, it was in a negative light. A "good Christian" would always give up a business commitment for a church committee meeting. Gradually, a picture of what he was dealing with emerged:

> The gap between the rhetoric of what the church was saying on
> Sunday and the reality of what was happening in my life on Monday
> was enormous.... [The church] was calling on me to serve as a disci-
> ple of Christ in the world without giving me any help on how to do

it. On the other hand, I got help in the form of affirmation, training, and even prayers for my service in the church as a Sunday school teacher, youth advisor, and church council member. For my Monday work as a Christian businessperson in a highly competitive environment, however, I received no affirmation, no training, no support, and no prayers. Nothing. There was absolutely no connection between Sunday and Monday.2

Diehl continues in his book to describe how he took on the task of trying to bridge this gap. With virtually no support from clergy, he began to read extensively in an attempt to construct a coherent worldview—one that encompassed the whole week. As he did so, he came to see that his declining mainline denomination's blind spot regarding work was but part of a larger blindness regarding the lived experiences of everyday life and personal experience:

It is clear that the mainline denominations, which are losing membership, tend to relate to society through institutional actions; the more fundamentalist denominations, which are gaining members, tend to relate to society through the actions of individual members.3

The culture of many denominations had become more institutional than personal. We expect people to fit their life experiences into our prefabricated religious molds and practices. We do not expect to use our training and vocation to illuminate the God present and working already in people's everyday world.

Another writer who seeks to reintegrate work and spirituality is Parker Palmer. In *The Active Life: A Spirituality of Work, Creativity, and Caring,* Palmer identifies a tendency for people to believe they have to choose between a life of work and action on the one hand and a monastic model of spirituality on the other. This can be a false choice, and through a series of stories Palmer describes ways the spiritual life can be viewed as an active life of involvement in everyday affairs.

Loren Mead also has sought to call attention to the current state of affairs. In his book *The Once and Future Church,* Mead argues that American society has entered a "post-Christendom era" in which the historical institutions no longer have significant influence. If the churches are to survive, they must serve people in the emerging reality rather than try to insulate themselves from the changes.

Some observers, then, have been calling for the churches to rethink what they are doing and to address recent changes in our culture. But some of the most interesting developments have been from the least expected quarter: secular organizational thinking.

A Hunger for Spirituality from Outside the Church

As the mainline churches had less and less to say to people in secular work, a curious thing began to happen. For decades, the prevailing model in management had been built on Taylor's rationalistic, mechanical, and industrial theories. The core assumption had been that human beings operated in a logical, predictable, and controllable fashion; the great visual icon of this culture was the organizational chart. Given enough rewards and obedience, all will go well. But starting in the late seventies, signs of a search for transcendence and spirituality began to appear in secular management, organizational development, and leadership literature:

• After a lifetime working in the human resources department of AT&T and working as a consultant for a variety of universities and business organizations, in 1977 Robert Greenleaf published *Servant Leadership,* asserting that the most effective leader is one who has the heart and attitude of a servant. Greenleaf, a lifelong Quaker, draws on his secular experience and also cites gospel stories and principles. The book grew steadily in popularity through the eighties and into the nineties.
• Meeting a hunger for people looking for meaningful work, in 1972 Richard Bolles began an annual publication for job seekers, *What Color Is Your Parachute.* Eventually, Bolles, an Episcopal priest, began adding an appendix to the end of each edition that encourages every job seeker to understand their life as a mission and their work as a spiritual vocation.
• In 1989, Stephen Covey published the popular book *The Seven Habits of Highly Successful People.* The book synthesizes a century of personal and professional growth literature and introduces spirituality as an important element of one of the habits. At the end of the book, Covey adds his own statement of faith, in which he discloses his spiritual perspective. His follow-up work, *First Things First,* develops more fully his ideas about the way working people can look to spirituality as a source of

direction and values. Appendixes in this book include not only the author's faith statement but a listing of "wisdom literature" for nurturing spirituality; the list includes the Bible, the Baghavad Gita, the I-Ching, and the Book of Mormon.

• In 1990, Peter Senge of the Sloan School of Management published *The Fifth Discipline,* which became the most influential book of its kind in the nineties. Senge described the first discipline "Personal Mastery," which includes a strong element of personal spirituality.

• Business periodicals began to notice the interest in spirituality. *Training Magazine,* a monthly journal for corporate trainers, made spirituality in the workplace its cover story in its June 1994 issue. In it, the editors noted the growing interest in Greenleaf and others who incorporate spirituality into discussions of organizational health. Similar articles have appeared in *Business Week* and *Industry Week.*

Clearly, a hunger for integration was being felt in the secular world. What is it that people in secular organizations are looking for when they explore spirituality? And what does integration look like in the lives of individual people?

To begin with, it is significant that the word being used to describe the object of this search was not "religion" or "faith" or even "morality" but "spirituality." Why "spirituality"?

The word "spirituality" has an interesting history. In essence, for centuries the word was used almost exclusively within the Catholic church. Protestants and nontraditional writers preferred words like "inner life." But beginning in the seventies, the word suddenly became popular across many traditions—Catholic, Protestant, Jewish, Native American, and Buddhist, as well as with many groups of people who had no ties with traditional faith communities. By the nineties, the word was used with great ease and little consistency by a great diversity of people. Such diversity was evidenced in my research project. One of the questions I asked the group was "What is spirituality?" Responses included the following:

> Spirituality suggests to me all aspects of God's creation, particularly the manner in which human beings attempt to better understand and love God.

> That within all of us that gives us hope—an inner glue.

For me, spirituality is the essence in my life that guides me to be the best I can be with the gifts I have been given. It inspires me with a drive to serve humanity that would not make sense otherwise. It is that other force in my life that is difficult to explain, but flows through me and continually provides miraculous, mysterious, and wondrous experiences that do not come from conscious effort. It is the touch of the divine that is in each one of us if we have faith and trust in a higher power...God...whatever name one wants to give it.

Spirituality to me is not some pious and righteous expression, but a humble walk with God. It means being in touch with your innermost feelings and understanding that you really can't separate the mind and body and spirit as easily as somehow we have in various religious traditions. There is a spiritual aspect to almost every part of human existence and that needs to be recognized. It is spiritual success that brings about real joy and not material success and clearly material success will not substitute. Spirituality is not the quantifiable aspect of life but is the essence of being.

Spirituality is my connection to the God who authored my life and this creation. It transcends the events of my days and the circumstances around me. As I grow spiritually all aspects of my vocational life come into closer accord with the behaviors of a Christian. My spirituality provides clear reason for my life and provides my peace and contentment regardless of other people or circumstances.

My ideas about spirituality were influenced by the great Jesuit scientist and theologian, Pierre Teilhard de Chardin, whose writings opened an enormous, wide window for me in the wake of the Second Vatican Council. Before Vatican II, we traditional Catholics believed that life on earth was a kind of cosmic basic training course, strewn with dangers and obstacles designed to trip us up on the road to heaven. Teilhard taught differently. Through his writing, I understood that God did not intend this world only as a test of our purity, but rather as an expression of his love; that we are meant to live actively, totally, in this world and in so doing to make it better for all whom we can touch; one's spiritual life need not be separate from one's earthly experiences—even politics.

Such responses indicate that the definition might not be clear but the word has great potency for people seeking to live integrated lives. The richness of the term is also revealed in the way people responded to a question asking them where they find inspiration:

> I am most renewed by those spiritual moments that could be hearing a traditional Latin mass in an old cathedral; sensing the stories and traditions that are in a tiny New Mexican mission; things that are in nature—the ocean at the jetty, spectacular, crisp, fall days, snow in the woods, Colorado aspen and streams, an early morning gift of seeing deer on the way to work, or how some morning's light gives a brief moment where everything is perfect. I take these as personal messages of encouragement and appreciation! People—true and honest conversations with people I am close to and admire; being a part of someone's personal victories over a challenge they may have; having the synergy of a work group just take off where they are self-propelled and excited about what they are doing; when perseverance rewards me with a breakthrough. I admit it: working inspires me and renews me when I am able to make a difference.
>
> I am inspired not only by traditional church activities, but by studying and reading the Bible and trying to come to a better understanding both on a mental and spiritual basis concerning my role in God's plan and His role in my professional and business life. I enjoy being in His creation and love power places that American natives used to go to and see why they feel they were closer to their creator in such environments. I enjoy my work at the bedside of patients and find inspiration in seeing them come to a point of healing and sometimes even when curing is not possible, seeing them deal with outcomes that are limited and even death in a heroic way and in a way where you can see their assurance because of their personal relationship with God. It is inspiring to see others in service to their fellow man and I like to see values put into action ...

What these responses suggest is that spirituality describes for many people the subjective side of what we often think of as "religion." Spirituality can include religion, and for many people is based in religion, but it is not bound by religious doctrine or cognitive categories. It can be found within religious institutions and traditions but is not controlled by them. It is often related to "faith," but faith often has a clear object—we "believe" *in* something; spirituality can have elements that are diffuse as well as clear. In my project, the participants could all agree to the following statement regarding the meaning of the word:

> Spirituality is a very difficult word to define. An adequate definition would include reference to a relationship with something beyond myself (known as "Creator," "God," "transcendent power," etc.) that is intangible but also real. It would recognize that spirituality is the source of one's values and meaning, a way of understanding the world, an awareness of my "inner self," and a means of integrating the various aspects of myself into a whole.

In short, spirituality might not be easy to pin down, but that elusiveness might be entirely appropriate, indicating that spirituality denotes something we will never be able to pin down. What is behind the power of the word in both secular and religious discussions is the hunger for integration and wholeness. Spirituality is that sense of the numinous in the everyday, the transcendent in the immanent, the divine in the ordinary.

Having wrestled with the meaning of the word, I do not pretend to have an inside track on any one definition. But the one I prefer is attributed to Thomas Aquinas: "Spirit means our capacity to relate to the totality of things."[4] In short, spirituality is our relationship to everything. For me and for many others, that includes God, specifically the God I have come to know through Christ. But it refers not just to what I *know* and *think* when I consciously reflect using theological categories and vocabulary, but, literally, to everything.[5]

Now, whether or not this enthusiasm for the word "spirituality" will endure is not certain. It is an indication, however, that many people who are close to the heart of contemporary working life are aware that there is a felt need for some kind of integration. If the church can speak to this need, people will deepen their relationship with the institution *and* this relationship will bear fruit in people's daily life. If the churches do not speak to this need, people will either live a disconnected life or they will search for integration apart from the churches.

This search for integration was certainly reflected in the microcosm of my research study. People in the study often spoke eloquently of how their deep values were originally formed in a religious institution. Sometimes that allegiance continued into adulthood. Often, however, the search took people beyond the bounds of institutional life into other traditions and areas—wherever integration could be found. A significant group in our society is yearning for integration. The question becomes: What does all this mean for the future of the historical churches? What choices do we have?

The Choice Before Us

I believe religious organizations have two choices.

• We can continue to focus entirely on the institutional concerns that are within our control. This would mean we could avoid the inconvenient and messy task of trying to understand the ambiguous and often complex reality of working life. There is a part of me that would prefer this option. I wouldn't have to admit my inability to integrate spirituality and work. I wouldn't have to examine any of my habits of mind. I could hope for the best. Like other communities under siege, we could pull up our draw-bridge, apportion the rations we have, and pray for divine deliverance.
• The other option is to adapt to the new realities. This does *not* mean accommodating the Gospel to secular thinking. It *does* mean looking for the meaning of the Gospel and the movement of the Holy Spirit in life as it really is, not as it should be or as it used to be. There are at least two reasons why we should do this.

First, it is at the heart of our duty to act as the "keepers of the grail." As committed lay people and clergy, we have been captivated by the voice of a living God as we have heard it through sacred Scriptures, tradition, community, and life experience. We have accepted a call to serve that God. So often, the discussion of spirituality in current secular literature lacks a sense of historical awareness and humility. It is often naive, shortsighted, and self-serving. Modern society needs to learn from the ancient wisdom that came from the same living presence we seek to serve. The search may go on without us, but it will be much more productive if we and our institutions become part of the search.

Second, we should take on the challenge because it arises out of our basic duty to serve our faith community, our neighborhoods, and the global community. The people we serve do not live in ancient Israel, in a prescientific age, or in a world guided by clearly defined religious principles or institutions. A recurring theme in the Hebrew prophets and in the ministry of Jesus is a challenge to religious leaders to remember that they have been given power to serve the people, not be served by them. How can we serve people if we do not attempt to understand and speak with insight to them as they are shaped by the workplace in our secularized, pluralistic society?

If we accept this challenge, we first need to take stock of our theology. How can it speak to people who work?

CHAPTER 2

A Practical Theology of Spirituality and Work

The Work of Theology

To be involved in ministry, lay or ordained, is to operate with some kind of theology. We respond to Scripture passages and life situations with basic operating assumptions about God. Such a theology might or might not be something we analyze in a systematic way. It might or might not be something we would want to articulate and defend in the presence of seminary professors. Practical theology in this sense is what Donald Schön has called "theory-in-action."[6] It's the patterns of thought we rely on to get through the week, through each crisis, through the real issues in our personal life. While I enjoy keeping up with theological debates and positions, I find much of my day-to-day theology doesn't make much use of academic categories. Yet that doesn't seem to matter to me as much now as it did when I was in seminary. What matters now is whether or not people's lives are being blessed—whether the imperfect things my church is doing enable ordinary people to bear fruit in their lives.

It is with this in mind that I want to offer a simple practical theology that tries to uncover the existing foundation for a living spirituality that honors both tradition and the experience of people who live and labor in a so-called secular workplace.

Creation as the Great Divine Work

Creation—meaning the sum of all the universe, seen and unseen—is basically good stuff. This is clearly the message of the first creation story in Genesis. God brings light, order, purpose, and blessing out of chaos. The work of God's hands is an expression of God's heart. Genesis tells a story of intentional, creative divine *work* in which God enables one layer of life after another to emerge out of chaos. On the sixth day, God looks at all that has been created (all the "work" God has done) and declares it to be not just adequate or neutral but "very good."

After these six days of labor comes the Sabbath. In our culture, this time of not working is often expressed as a weekend, a time to escape and forget work. But this is not the case in the Genesis story. For God, the Sabbath is meant to be a time to savor what one has done and to see it in perspective of one's total life. This was to be the lesson for Israel: use the Sabbath not to escape work, but to appreciate it.

The theme of the blessedness of creation is a pervasive one in the Hebrew Scriptures. Proverbs 8 contains a poetic celebration of the active presence of wisdom in the world, concluding with the words:

When he established the heavens, I was there,
    when he drew a circle on the face of the deep,
when he made firm the skies above,
    when he established the fountains of the deep,
when he assigned to the sea its limit,
    so that the waters might not transgress his command,
when he marked out the foundations of the earth,
    then I was beside him, like a master worker;
and I was daily his delight,
    rejoicing before him always
rejoicing in his inhabited world
    and delighting in the human race.

(27–31)

Wisdom is not just some mental activity; wisdom is the genius behind the work of creation, and it is a cause for delight.

This belief that the material world is divine work is also evident in the most basic statements of the creeds. The Apostles' Creed begins with the first principle: "I believe in God the Father almighty, maker of heaven and earth."

Modern science, although it does not address questions of divine presence, has nevertheless exposed us to more and more sources for

wonder and amazement. To be sure, the universe has its terrors. But
when we see a child born or grasp the vitality of quantum physics or
appreciate the interrelationships within ecological systems or consider
the energy present in a quasar, we find ourselves in an appropriate state
of awe. It's all a miracle. From a spiritual perspective, the miracle is a
result of divine labor and work.

This aspect of the presence of God in creation is, of course, one of
the most deeply held beliefs among parishioners. It is reflected in the
popularity of hymns like "How Great Thou Art," "This Is My Father's
World," and "Morning Has Broken." This is why people put flowers on
altars. This is what is behind Sunday school lessons in which children
put bean seeds in cups and draw pictures of butterflies that once were
caterpillars. The tangible power of this truth has led people to build in-
numerable church camps by lakes and in forests because people instinc-
tively know that to be "in nature" is to be "close to God." It is the re-
generating power of the truth that draws so many to spend vacations "out
in nature."

All of this, then, affirms the basic belief that creation is essentially
good and a dependable resource for spiritual empowerment.

Humanity as a Divine Work and the Divine Work of Humanity

Humanity is one aspect of creation. We are one of an incredible number
of species living on the earth. The first creation story in Genesis describes the emergence of humanity, male and female, as the culmination
of life's development. We are created in the image of God. Humanity is
the great reach of the created order, an ambitious leap into new possibilities. We are not God, but we are in dialogue with God.

Looking further in Genesis, we find in the second creation story another affirmation of the importance of humanity. Yahweh creates Adam
to bring further order to the earth. Eve is created in honor and with purpose. The theme is a recurring one. Psalms like Psalm 8 celebrate both
the creation and the human place in it. Humanity is, put simply, a great
and divine work.

Humanity is itself a divine work, and it also is given work to do. In
the Garden of Eden story, we find Israel's understanding of that work:

"The LORD God took the man and put him in the garden of Eden to till it and keep it" (Gen. 2:15). God has performed the initial labors of creation and now calls humanity to be a coworker, a steward. This labor is an opportunity to share in the divine life and activity.

This theme of work as a blessing is echoed elsewhere in the Hebrew Scriptures. Psalm 104 provides a panoramic view of creation and humanity's place in it. After noting the beauty of the mountains and streams along with the splendor of mountain goats and birds, the writer declares:

> You cause the grass to grow for the cattle,
>   and plants for people to use,
> to bring forth food from the earth,
>   and wine to gladden the human heart,
> oil to make the face shine,
>   and bread to strengthen the human heart.
>
> (14–15)

Going on to recognize the place of cedar trees, storks, wild goats, the moon and sun, the writer again finds humanity:

> The young lions roar for their prey,
>   seeking their food from God.
> When the sun rises, they withdraw
>   and lie down in their dens.
> People go out to their work
>   and to their labor until the evening.
> O LORD, how manifold are your works!
>   In wisdom you have made them all;
>   the earth is full of your creatures.
>
> (21–23)

Again, humanity is part of the created order and the "work" of humanity is part of a cosmic pattern of life.

The value of meaningful work is again reflected in the life of parishioners: the experience of work is often rewarding. The apple farmers I got to know during my seven years in Washington are notoriously hard workers. Some of that is due to the financial pressures of farming. But there is also great satisfaction in using determination, ingenuity, and sheer effort to cooperate with nature and bring forth tons of delicious fruit. Teachers and school administrators are understandably weary, but still they enjoy using their skill and training to enable a child to learn a concept or grow through a personal challenge. Engineers take delight in well-designed systems, carpenters in square corners and snug joints, bank officers in helping clients resolve financial anxieties. Pastors have even been known to find satisfaction in a sermon that went well, a counseling relationship that brought new hope for someone, or a healing that has occurred through the caring of a parish. In these moments, we realize the original spiritual purpose of our labor. We labor to bless.

Of course, all humanity is not without problems. Following the second creation story, Adam's original blessed state of work becomes flawed through disobedience. For that lack of trust in God, work will seem more like a curse:

> And to the man he said, "Because you have listened to the voice of your wife, and have eaten of the tree about which I commanded you, 'You shall not eat of it,' cursed is the ground because of you; in toil you shall eat of it all the days of your life; thorns and thistles it shall bring forth for you; and you shall eat the plants of the field. By the sweat of your face you shall eat bread until you return to the ground, for out of it you were taken; you are dust, and to dust you shall return." (Gen. 3:17-19)

Anyone who has been frustrated by the futility and frustration of work can identify with this passage. Farmworkers, teachers, engineers, and even pastors can know this kind of futility. Though the story is 3,000 years old, it speaks to what can happen in work.

A similar theme is present in Ecclesiastes. Here the writer describes what it is like to accomplish many personal and material goals through work. There can be great satisfaction in such work. But we can also get to a point in life when we accomplish much and feel little. In our time, this often surfaces in the proverbial midlife crisis, or the sense many people have late in life that they have missed something profound.

The curse on Adam and the words of Ecclesiastes can lead us to a pessimistic view of work. Work can seem like a necessary evil, a curse. This theme is an important one, and it fits with many people's experience. How often people go to work with a sense of dread! A couple I was counseling recently was being worn down by the wife's overbearing boss. Another couple's marriage had been torn apart by the financial and interpersonal stresses they experienced as their business went through bankruptcy. A young college graduate recently dropped by with harrowing tales of the dysfunctional patterns of an investment company where he had worked for two years. I have known farmers who worked six and a half days a week for a year in their orchard only to have falling apple prices leave them with $2400 in annual earnings. Lack of trust, greed, injustice, and illusions about what is lasting in life can make work a curse and a futile endeavor. But that is not the divine intent. Work is meant to be our participation in divine creative action. It can be a curse, but ultimately it is meant to be a blessing.

The Work of Jesus

From a Christian perspective, these themes of intended blessing and the human response come into vivid focus in the life and work of Jesus.

One of the basic Christian affirmations is that God was "incarnate" in Jesus; as John's gospel puts it, "The Word became flesh and dwelt among us." The incarnation is a great affirmation of the goodness of material reality. In the gospel stories, God does not float above human existence. God's child become human through the silent work in Mary's womb and the painful "work" of her labor in Bethlehem. Jesus is not above work; he is a carpenter. He learns from his father how to work in a creative manner with his hands and wood. In this manual labor he helps sustain the needs of his community and in turn sustains himself and his family and receives the fruit of others' labor.

At some point, Jesus becomes aware of his call to ministry. People will forever speculate on what his "inner experience" must have been like, but it is clear that he became grounded in an extraordinary awareness of God. This awareness did not draw him away from work, however. Instead, it made clear what his work was to be.

He began work in Galilee. One aspect of his work was healing, making whole. This he did time and time again, often in direct violation of laws that forbade work on the Sabbath. Another aspect of his work was teaching. He did this primarily through parables, stories, and direct reflections on everyday experience. So it is that he compares finding the kingdom of God to the work of a pearl merchant or a woman cleaning house. He speaks of laborers in vineyards and taking risks by investing

talents. Inherent in this aspect of his teaching is an assumption that
everyday working life is a rich arena for gaining insight about the presence of God. He does not tell people their work is unnecessary or unspiritual; he tells them instead to become aware of their relationship to
God in the midst of all they do.

Jesus' ministry is also significant in light of *where* it occurs. He
spends very little time within the confines of places of worship. He is
blessed in the temple as an infant and spends several days there when he
is twelve. The gospels note that, as an adult, he often was teaching in the
synagogues as part of the regular Sabbath service. But the vast majority
of his time he is not within those presumably "sacred," protective walls.
Instead he is out in the midst of "secular" life—fishing docks, wheat
fields, tax collector's homes, and public squares. The setting for two of
his most familiar parables, the good Samaritan and the prodigal son, are
not in a temple but on a dangerous highway and a family farm. Increasingly, Jesus confronts the institutions that exist more to be served than
to serve. His arrival in Jerusalem is marked by turning over the money
changers' tables and publicly ridiculing the religious authorities. His last
appearance in a place of worship is before the Sanhedrin, where he is
condemned. Taken as a whole, he seems to be more at home in the places
where everyday people work than in the places where the religious authorities work. His very presence "outside the walls" of the religious
institutions is an act of divine affirmation of the value of everyday life
and ordinary people.

Although Jesus does much to affirm everyday life, he also demon-
strates that anything which violates God's intent for blessing can be
challenged. He is, in Niebuhr's phrase, a "transformer of culture."[7] His
prophetic passions reveal a pure standard by which to assess life, yet the
specific effects on people's working life varies with each individual. So
it is that he tells the rich young ruler that he must sell all he has to find
the kingdom. He tells the story of Dives and Lazarus to suggest that the
rich who do not have compassion on the poor will regret it in the life to
come. Clearly, he rails against anyone who identifies wealth or position
as the ultimate source of meaning.

Yet taken as a whole, his message is not meant to diminish people's
livelihoods. He seems to be interested instead in setting right each person's relationship with work and material goods. For instance, his encounter with Zacchaeus does not lead the tax collector to abandon his

profession. Instead Zacchaeus shows that "salvation has come to his house today" by giving away half of what he owns, making reparations to those he cheated, and resolving to make all his future business dealings honest. In Jesus' exchange with the Roman centurion who comes asking for healing for his servant, Jesus does not require the centurion to leave his position or authority in order to receive grace. Recognizing the man's humility and compassion, he lifts him up to the crowd as the example of a righteous person.

Jesus, then, was a product of divine labor. He himself was a laborer. Much of what he does affirms the importance of "secular," everyday life. He brings to working people a challenge to examine life in terms of the vivid reality of God. But he does that not to bring chaos into their lives but to bring to human life the depth of blessing that is at the heart of the created order.

These aspects of Jesus' person and work, in my experience, are not always recognized in church life. Anytime I have referred to Jesus' working life in a study or service, I have sensed a sharpened interest in those present. It is a great thing when people grasp that stories like those of the good Samaritan and the prodigal son are not about pious church life but about common situations in which we can find the kingdom of God. Yet moments in which we recognize Jesus honoring everyday life are rare. Caught up in theologies that tend to see Jesus as otherworldly and the church as separate from everyday life, it is hard for many of us to really accept the possibility that Jesus sanctified the world of ordinary women and men as he found them in their workplaces and homes. We have been taught that his exclusive desire was to provide a remedy for our "sin-sick soul" instead of bringing power and wisdom to our entire experience. In short, the work of Jesus is to uncover God's presence and possibilities in all aspects of our life.

The Work of the Spirit

The Holy Spirit is the great laborer of creation. We find the Spirit moving over the face of chaotic waters in the opening verses of Genesis, doing the preparatory work for what is to come. The psalmist celebrates the Spirit as the source of life, reflecting on the full range of living species and declaring: "When you send forth your spirit, they are created; and you renew the face of the ground" (104:30). We find the Spirit inspiring judges like Deborah, who must do the hard administrative and judicial work required to lead a community. The Spirit lays hold of Isaiah and Jeremiah, giving them vocation and purpose. According to Luke, the Spirit makes possible Jesus' conception in Mary and fills Jesus when he begins his ministry in Nazareth. In John's gospel, the Spirit is promised as the great counselor and advocate who will work tirelessly and relentlessly to enable Jesus' followers to grow in knowledge and love. The Spirit comes at Pentecost and begins working in the disciples' lives, guiding them, prodding them, enabling them to accomplish works of healing.

Like Jesus, the Spirit does not seem confined to religious institutions. The Spirit speaks to Philip on the road from Jerusalem to Gaza (Acts 8:29) and gives Peter a vision when he is on a rooftop waiting for lunch in Joppa (Acts 10:19). As stated in the Nicene Creed, the Spirit is "the Lord, the giver of life" and seems to be anxious to give that life anywhere.

To speak of the Holy Spirit can be more challenging than speaking of God or Jesus. Just how the Spirit is understood as present in people's lives varies, not only among individuals but also within worshipping communities. If asked to describe specifically experiences of the presence of the Spirit, people can often come up with a fascinating list: the birth of a child, peace following the death of a loved one, a reflective moment in a worship service. In my experience, at least 80 percent of these experiences happen outside church property and activities. This is significant for a spirituality relevant to working life. People find the Spirit as they ride alone on a tractor, kneel down to listen to a preschool student, or turn away from a computer monitor for a moment's reflection. Sometimes, of course, people have to leave their work environment to "find the Spirit." Some use a lunch hour to sit in a chapel or take a walk in a park. Others need to be with friends. But wherever people are, the Spirit is there, working, hovering, brooding, yearning to bless and instruct.

The Work of the Church

If we understand creation, humanity, Jesus, and the Spirit to be specific expressions of divine work, the role of the church can take on new meaning.

The biblical story begins without the presence of any institutions. First there is God, then creation, then people who enter into relationship with God. Israel forms as a community in the Exodus experience and is given structure at Sinai. The early years in the promised land are marked by an avoidance of settled institutions. Soon, however, both the temple and the monarchy arrive. From the beginning, these institutions play ambiguous roles in the life of the people. At their best, they act to preserve the divine story and wisdom and become avenues for God's activity and blessing. At their worst, they place their own existence and power ahead of the needs of the people. It is in these latter times that the prophets rise to bring God's words of judgment.

In the New Testament, the church itself is not formally established during Jesus' life. After his resurrection, the community forms and seeks ways of organizing itself that will allow it to accomplish Jesus' mission. The history of the church since then has been like that of the temple. Churches have blessed and protected many lives, fed countless people, built thousands of hospitals, and challenged oppressive governments. Yet the church has also lost its way, becoming focused on its own existence and power rather than God's.

This ambivalent character of churches is certainly reflected in popular experience. People often find the church a great source of inspiration, community, and selfless service. But people lose interest or respect when any church places selfish aims first or is not ready to adapt to contemporary needs.

Certainly, one proper role of the church is to be a "holy place," a place and community that has the specific function of being a sanctuary dedicated to the glory and service of God. No business or public institution has as its primary function the proclamation of the Gospel and the administration of sacraments. The church is the place where our spiritual traditions, practices, and understandings are preserved and renewed. It is the place where the passages of life—birth, marriage, death—are recognized as having transcendent meaning. But if it is to be a place truly dedicated to facilitate the work of God, it must have a broader purpose.

One image that may be useful is that of the church as a base camp for a hiking expedition. Scott Peck uses this image for marriage: a marriage is a base camp in which two people share common life. From there, they move out to explore their own paths, always returning to base camp for rest, renewal, and restoration. This is a fruitful image for the church. The church is a base camp in which a community of people gather to reflect on life, be reminded of their identity, and make plans for exploration. From there, each person goes out during the week to take on that part of the mountain that is theirs to explore. The base camp exists to serve the climbing team. In itself, it is neither the goal of the expedition nor the mountain itself. The value of this image is that it affirms the importance of the community and institution but it does not mistake the institution for the central reality. The hikers don't exist for the good of the base camp. The base camp exists for the good of the hikers.

This perspective on the nature of the church is reflected in a comment I once heard at a Saturday evening mass. The priest was speaking about Jesus' ministry and the role of the church. He said, "The church is *not* the place we experience God. We can experience God all through the week. The church is the place we gather once a week to *celebrate* the ways in which God has been with us the other six days."

The implications of this view of the church's role for working people is clear. The church needs to focus on its timeless tasks: it is to be a place of worship, education, and community. But it also needs to evaluate how well it is empowering people for the work on the mountain those other six days. The church exists for the people, not the reverse. People deserve our help in making sense of all seven days.

Moving Toward Integration

If we look to Scripture for an understanding of work, we find that work is meant to be a gift. God's gift of the world is accomplished through divine labor. Humanity has work to do, and though such work can become like a curse, that is not God's intention. Jesus' work is to bring the kingdom on God to people where they live and labor, and the Holy Spirit forever continues helping us to accomplish this task. The church is meant to serve the purposes of God and the people of God. The church as leaders and community can do this through preaching and worship, through counseling and spiritual direction, through education, and through our leadership as a whole. If our souls have found rest in God, then it is time to get to work.

CHAPTER 3

In the Study and Sanctuary: The Work of Preaching

Preaching as Seen from the Pew

Imagine yourself sitting in the pews on a Sunday morning. You hear the text read. You hear it interpreted to clarify its meaning in its original setting. Then you hear how it comes into play today. You hear a story about how it is embodied in your personal relationship with God. Yes, you say, that makes sense, that resonates with what my life is like. And then you hear a story about how it relates to the activities of your church. That also rings true. It reinforces why you feel good about being a part of your church. The sermon ends with a prayer. You sing a hymn. You come forward for the bread and wine. You sing another hymn, receive the benediction, and go out to coffee hour looking for friends. Later you go home and feel good about having gone to church. The world seems a little clearer and God a little closer.

On Monday morning you return to work. No Scripture is read here. No hymns or prayers. You greet your coworkers, some with affection and some with basic courtesy. But the day's work begins. You find yourself thinking back with longing for the weekend, a time when everything seemed less stressful, more meaningful. You think of the issues facing you: the work you're involved in, the people you work with, the person who is your supervisor. It's a different world here. In fact, sometimes you feel like you're living in two worlds. You take a deep sigh and get to work.

Roses vs. Mulch

In my denomination, preaching is often the center of church life. When pastors are seeking a position, they are often judged on sermon quality and delivery. Week after week, the sermon is a common topic for conversation at the door to the sanctuary. When I go home on Sundays, it's hard not to evaluate how well a sermon went based on the reaction of parishioners. Did they seem to like what I had to offer? Or did they avoid saying anything? With all this emphasis on preaching, most pastors desire to create sermons that gather blue ribbons for eloquence and beauty. We are tempted to create beautiful roses.

In the early years of my work, strong preaching seemed to be the key to a meaningful ministry. But as I went on, I began to recognize that the production of great homiletical roses might not be what God has called us to do. I have heard it said that good preaching is not an act in which someone creates a rhetorical rose for people to admire. Preaching is creating a mulch that can be worked into the soil of people's lives. It is in people's lives that the true roses appear. What does it profit a preacher to have people leave a service admiring the pastor's eloquence if they do not find a new appreciation for the presence and call of God that permeates every aspect of their lives? I developed that conviction from a steady accumulation of experiences:

• This lesson began to bear down on me when, five years out of seminary, I began work in rural Washington. It was an area where people did not read fancy journals or worry too much about *Time* magazine or the *New York Times*. What was good preaching there?

• In Washington, I served on a denominational committee that was working with a conflicted church. While waiting for a meeting to begin, one member began reminiscing about a prior pastor who had done much to build up this congregation. This person believed every sermon should be "90 percent application"—that everyone leaving a worship service should have a concrete idea of how they could apply the text's theme in the week ahead. I reacted with both interest and fear—fear because I realized I wouldn't know *how* to spend 90 percent of my preaching time suggesting how a passage could have a practical effect on people's lives.

• As part of one of my doctoral seminars, I did a sociological study of one of the large, nondenominational churches that has grown so rapidly in the last decade. At one service I attended, the preacher certainly wasn't creating a rhetorical rose; his way of interpreting Scripture was certainly not mine. When he was getting to the end, he looked at his watch and told the congregation, "OK, our time is almost up, so let's talk about how we can apply this to our life. Take your pencil—or scab one from someone nearby ("scab" is California surf talk for "procure"), and write down in your Bible these three points...." I was aware of how the educated, careful part of me thought it was a rather sloppy—and perhaps presumptuous—way to end a sermon. But the deeper part of me—the part of me that hungers to have a closer relationship with a living God—wanted to push aside those reservations, "scab" a pencil, and preserve something that just might be important for my life.

• On the rare Sundays when I am away on vacation or study leave, I try to notice my own criteria for choosing a church. I don't really want to go hear someone who is simply well-read or smart or who has good diction. I don't really care what the denomination is or what the building looks like. I want to hear someone who, in a clear and direct way, can help me find the living God in the here and now. As Garrison Keillor has put it: We don't go to church to hear lectures about ethics. We want to hear just one thing that the preacher has heard from the Spirit.

These experiences gradually caused me to change my approach to preaching. I became less interested in growing roses and more interested in making mulch.

St. Paul writes: "When I came to you, brothers and sisters, I did not come proclaiming the mystery of God to you in lofty words or wisdom.... My speech and my proclamation were not with plausible words of wisdom, but with a demonstration of the Spirit and of power, so that your faith might rest not on human wisdom but on the power of God" (1 Cor. 2:1-5). Paul wasn't into roses. Paul valued spiritual mulch. The mulch we all need is to see how the transcendent God, the risen Christ, appears in the soil of our everyday lives.

If we want preaching to be an act of mulch making for people's lives, then we need to recognize the soil people live in. In great measure, that soil includes the world of work. So the question becomes: How does preaching become useful for people who spend so much of their life in a secular workplace?

Designing a Strategy for Preaching about Work

Before getting into the particulars of preaching about work, I want to
make clear my assumptions. One has to do with what really happens in
the work of preaching. One of my seminary professors, Randy Nichols,
made the persuasive argument that what is most important in preaching
is not what is said in any one sermon—what its particular point or theme
may be. Instead, it is what the communications scholar George Gerbner
would call "the systemic message features" of a whole series of sermons.[8]
Gerbner's insight is that every message has implicit in it the answer to
four questions: what is, what is important, what is right, and what is related to what else. If we studied someone's preaching over a two-year
period with those questions in mind, we would begin to see the preacher's
worldview emerge. We would be able to guess what he or she believes is
real, what is important, what is right, and what is related to what else. As
Nichols urged us to ask, Over a long period of time, do preachers really
talk about a world that ordinary people recognize?

When I began to become aware of the importance of work in people's lives, this insight came back to haunt me. I reflected on what I had
been saying. What was real to me? God. What is important? Faith and
living life in response to grace. What is right? Doing what God wants us
to do. Not bad, so far. But the last question was the tough one. What does
all this relate to? I had to admit: primarily, life in the church. Fidelity to
the institution and its programs. In William Diehl's terms, the Gospel I
interpreted was mostly about Sunday morning. I realized I hadn't always
been "on the road" with people the way Jesus was. Thinking of Gerbner's
last question, I began to wonder what it would be like to preach in a way
that would give a different answer to that fourth question. What would it
be like to preach for two years in such a way that, if someone in my
church was asked "What do the sermons at your church relate to?" they
might answer "They relate to the real-life world I live and work in."

Now, at first take, this was exciting to me. But as I decided to try to
begin this journey, I became aware I really didn't know how to do it very
well. I'd always been taught to look at a text for its theological theme,
not what it has to say about work. Most of my illustrations came from
reading and conversations that had to do with subjects of interest to me.
Where would I find stories about working life? When faced with ethical
dilemmas, I had always thought it was enough simply to affirm an

abstract moral principle. How could I find my way down to the less tidy reality of work situations?

What this involved for me was a shift in habits and perceptions, a major course adjustment. I often felt awkward and wondered if the effort would be worth it. But like many other changes we make, the enterprise turned out to be not as bad as I had expected.

In essence, I came to think of preaching as having two basic elements: the message of the text, and illustrations that show how the message makes a difference in the way we live. Like many other colleagues, I have developed a simple procedure for preparation:

• Early in the week, I try to study the Scripture text to establish its core message or point. If it has multiple points, I choose the one that seems most fruitful for the spiritual journey of my congregation and decide how to express it.

• I then begin to look for illustrations or stories that will show how this theme gets put into action in people's lives.

Let's look first at work issues as they are already present in Scripture.

Reading Scripture with Work in Mind

One of the rewarding aspects of ministry is working with ancient stories that have the capacity to be endlessly revealing. As Paul Ricouer has said, great texts are great because they have "a surplus of meaning."9 At any particular point in our life, or in any situation we find ourselves, we consciously or unconsciously have certain questions or issues that we bring to the interpretive process. Like a cornucopia filled with the harvest of the land, a greater variety of meanings can be found in sacred stories than common sense would suppose. Texts we thought we knew can speak to us again and again in new ways. This aspect of Scripture is certainly demonstrated when we bring to biblical texts issues of work and concerns that arise outside of church culture.

As we preach through a given year, we can simply keep an eye out to see how work relates to people's spiritual life. In chapter 1, we noted how work plays a significant role in the stories of some major figures of the Bible. Consider again those stories and others and how the theme of work is present but not always recognized:

• Adam and Eve's offspring, Cain and Abel, are initially defined primarily by their different vocations ("Now Abel was a keeper of sheep and Cain a tiller of the ground," Gen. 4:2). When God does not accept Cain's offering, which his work has produced, Cain's jealousy leads him to murder his brother. After recognizing the awkward issue of a God who rejects certain kinds of work, we might consider whether there is an important lesson about what can develop when the value of people's work is not recognized.

• Generations later, Abraham and Sarah's great-grandson Joseph achieves power and influence not simply because he possessed spiritual knowledge but because of his ability to apply that knowledge effectively as a high ranking civil servant in Pharaoh's court. When we speak of Joseph, perhaps we need to say he is a great person in the way he works *through* his government service, not apart from it.

• Moses has a variety of ways to earn his daily bread. While the main theme of his life is his fidelity to God, this is also a story that suggests it is OK to "change careers" as we respond to the topsy-turvy life of faith.

• Ruth finds a new life for both herself and her mother-in-law through the workplace. It is in her work as a gleaner in the barley field that she encounters Boaz, a farmer who grants her special privileges. This encounter leads to romance and marriage. David's great-grandparents, then, find each other not in a temple but in a field where they both make their living. The story implies we can see a "secular" workplace as a place where "divine" things can happen.

• The prophet Amos works in agriculture as a pruner of sycamore trees. This rural work experience allows him to see the inequities of the social system in his time. Grounded in his faith and open to God's voice, he becomes a powerful prophet against economic exploitation. How often does our working situation help us to see such social inequities?

• Zacchaeus, like Matthew, is a tax collector. Jesus' encounter with Zacchaeus does not result in Zacchaeus changing careers but instead in a decision to remain in this career with a new view of his ethical responsibilities.

• Luke is a physician who seems to practice his profession while being a vital member of the early church.

• The parable of the prodigal son is surely about many things, including forgiveness, renewal, and the conflict of grace and responsibility. But the way Jesus tells the story, it is when he is in a depressing work situation—feeding pigs as a foreigner—that the younger son "comes to himself" and decides to return home for an entry-level job on his father's estate. How might work situations be means of revealing aspects of our relationship with God?

• Paul recognizes a slave woman is being exploited by men who care nothing for her own integrity. He sees her vocation as unacceptable and uses his power to free her, despite the consequences and retaliations from her employers (Acts 16:19).

The homiletical point here is that when one is preaching on such texts, it is important to recognize issues of work present in a story. People need to hear that the Bible is not just about life in faith communities; it is about people who often encounter God in the workplace. Work issues develop naturally from a text when we interpreters are ready to recognize them. As we begin to interpret a passage for a congregation, we can identify work elements and reflect on their meaning. If we do this over a period of months and years, we will help people see how the biblical worldview resonates with the real world—that work and faith are not separate elements of our lives but part of a whole. But this is not the only way we can connect spirituality and work. We can also do it by the kind of illustrations we use.

Illustrations that Apply to the Workplace

Helping people understand what a text means for them often includes reflecting on the theme and then making a transition to suggest the way this theme applies to everyday life. Illustrations form the core of the application. Having heard the point, the listeners can hear an illustration, and we hope they will then say to themselves, "Yes, now I see how that might work in my life." If, for instance, the passage's theme is that we should put our relationship with God above all else, the sermon will also ask, how will I see specific life situations differently in light of that? (We are answering Gerbner's question, What is related to what else?)

I have come to think of illustrations as falling into five basic categories. These categories are like a series of concentric circles that start with our personal awareness and expand outward into our relationships in the world. The categories are

1. our personal spiritual journeys and relationship with God;
2. our relationships with other people, particularly within families;
3. our work together in the church;
4. experiences and challenges in the workplace;
5. our actions in the community and world as agents of reconciliation and justice.

As part of my sermon preparation, I try to find at least one illustration within each category. Of course, not all texts will make connections with all five categories. But it is surprising how often a given passage can be seen to speak to each of these five areas. From a communication point of view, using five illustrations would probably be too many; three seems to be a practical norm. And, to be sure, some illustrations are so rich and poignant that they can serve as the sole illustration for that day. But for the garden-variety Sunday message, my rule of thumb is to try to use three. And I have set a goal of often having at least *one* of them be from the work category.

We can look at three common texts to see how illustrations can function: the Twenty-Third Psalm, the parable of the prodigal son, and Romans 8:28.

The Twenty-Third Psalm is about our relationship with God and God's role as both our shepherd and our gracious host. The six verses offer a rich variety of points that can relate to the various aspects of our life. An illustration from the first category might be about someone whose life changed when he accepted Christ as shepherd. An illustration focusing on the second verse (in which "righteousness," in the original Hebrew sense, means fulfilling relationships) might tell about a family that was transformed when one of the family members began honoring their relationships. In the church category, I might find a reference to a particular church community acting as a comforting presence when someone had to walk through the dark valley of the death of a loved one. On the work level, I could tell a story about how an organization took seriously the need for people to have times of rest and reflection (green pastures and still waters) and found increased satisfaction among its workers. Or I might know of a situation in which someone in a supervisorial role was effective because she started seeing herself more as a "shepherd" than a "supervisor." Finally, on the world community level, the illustration might be about someone who has seen all humanity as "the sheep" under God's care and tries to be an agent of care.

From those five illustrations, I would usually pick three. I might make my choice based on the quality of the illustration. Or I might be keeping an eye on what is happening in my community or world events. Or I might make a fairly arbitrary decision. But I try not to chose illustrations because they are the only ones I thought of; I try to push my imagination to find five and to stretch specifically in the direction of work. Developing illustrations does not always have to be a solo task. In some congregations, a lay task force works with the preacher to develop the services and sermons for a season. Sermons then can easily include stories about task force members' experiences in the workplace or elsewhere.

As another example, take the prodigal son/elder brother/loving-father-caught-in-the-middle parable from Luke. In my experience as both a preacher and listener, the story often finds embodiment in four of the five illustration categories. The parable is illustrated with a story about someone who has returned to God and found God's grace running down the road in greeting. It might be illustrated with a story about the struggle of parents to know how to respond to "wayward" children and their brooding, responsible siblings. A story might lift up the need for churches to model the father's forgiveness toward undeserving people, even when being forgiving doesn't seem fair. Sometimes the parable is illustrated by citing issues of forgiveness among rival ethnic groups and nations. The other category—the issue of how it applies to the workplace—is rarely touched. Yet how often the issue raised in the parable can come into play in work! An illustration that takes place in a secular workplace and that addresses the tensions involved in forgiveness can be highly appropriate. The story could be about what it is it like to work in an organization in which the supervisor has the father's kind of grace-based love for people. Or, conversely, it could be what is it like to work in an "elder brother organization"—where the emphasis is all on duty and no one believes in the possibility that people can be transformed.

We can look at one other example, the much-beloved verse from Romans 8:28: "We know that all things work together for good for those who love God, who are called according to his purpose." In the personal category, we can probably find a story in which someone was faced with a personal tragedy but was able to eventually find blessings growing out of the situation. In the relational category, we can call to mind a story of a family that was able to pull together to overcome a challenge by believing God was with them. As a church, we might describe the way in which a support group for widows and widowers became a powerful source of support and new hope. And in relation to the world, we might remind everyone of someone like Bishop Tutu who used apartheid to clarify the power of the Gospel in South Africa. But, again, we can take one more step and imagine what the passage might mean for someone at work. What immediately comes to mind is the stories of people who lose a job through downsizing or defense cutbacks. This can be particularly harrowing if it means a family must experience all the stresses of unemployment or relocation. But the text has a powerful message for someone in that situation: God might not have "willed" the change, but God is fundamentally focused on helping that person and family find a way to some new possibilities through the situation.

Certainly these texts can speak powerfully to the human situation *without* referring to the work environment. And it might be unrealistic to expect we can find a good illustration from the working environment for every text. *But imagine what might happen if on most Sundays people were able to go to church and see ways Scripture can open up God's presence and purposes in their "Monday" reality of work.* What would that be like for people as they move through their week and as they form images of how God might be at work in the world?

Once we recognize the significance of including work issues in our preaching, we need a process for gathering useful stories and information.

Gathering Insights and Illustrations

First, the preacher needs to be culturally literate in the world of work. How much is involved here depends on the experience of the particular pastor. Those who have come into the ministry following a career in secular work might have an advantage: they might be able to call on years of experience and contacts outside the church world for illustrative material. Those of us whose experience outside the church is minimal might need to develop some ongoing ways to gain such literacy.

One way to do this that is fairly easy and highly rewarding is to tap into the experiences of the people in our congregation. We can simply develop the habit of asking people about what their work is like—how they feel about it, and how they might see issues of faith come to play in the workplace. While more will be said about this in chapter 4, suffice it to say that people's response to such questions is very helpful. I inevitably hear stories about tangible ways in which someone in the workplace has expressed faith, ethical dilemmas people encounter, and people's feelings of emptiness and discouragement as well as expressions of joy and satisfaction. Such stories often stick with me, and I look for opportunities to use them.

Another way to gather relevant illustrations is simply through the age-old practice of observing such issues as they arise in the media. At the seminary I attended, we were often reminded that all preachers should preach with the Bible in one hand and the daily newspaper in the other. Most daily newspapers, as well as weekly news magazines like *Time* and *Newsweek*, include sections on political news, human interest stories, and sports, as well a business section. *All* sections can provide stories that embody themes helpful in illustrating a point.

I also have found it helpful to make use of the periodicals that focus on issues of business and working life. *Fortune, Forbes, Business Week,* and the *Wall Street Journal* often provide surprising, relevant stories about issues in the workplace that can be touched on in a preaching season. Influential community publications can be useful sources of illustrations and issues. When I lived in a rural area of Washington state, I read *The Good Fruit Grower;* now that I live in an academic community, I read *The Chronicle of Higher Education*. Most publications designed for pastors—the biblical, theological, denominational, and church management journals—are helpful for doing our own work, but they are not always the best sources of illustrative material that is helpful when preaching to people who work outside the church. Such material needs to be found elsewhere.

Another source of illustrations are the newsletters, periodicals, and web sites being published by organizations that are trying to infuse the workplace with more spirituality. *The Servant Leader*, published quarterly by the Greenleaf Center highlights stories of public and private organizations that are seeking to act in the servant role. The New Leaders Press publishes a bimonthly newsletter that features interviews and articles that involve the current search for working organizations that are more humane and ethical. The monthly *Business Ethics* magazine has a similar focus.

A fourth source of insight and illustrations are the books being written about the issues of spirituality, work, and secular leadership. As noted in chapter 1, the work of people like Peter Senge, Stephen Covey, and Robert Greenleaf is not only helpful to our own work as organizational leaders but also for the illustrations that are used. Covey, in particular, makes simple, basic truths become clear through anecdote and example. His is, in my experience, good and useful material. Tom Chappel, CEO of Tom's of Maine, has written *The Soul of a Business*, an account of the midlife crisis that led him first to seminary and then to a renewal of his company. He even asked the board of directors to read Martin Buber. A helpful and succinct collection in which lay people reflect on the role spirituality plays in their secular jobs is *Faith Goes to Work: Reflections from the Marketplace* by Robert J. Banks. Banks also includes a list of resources that explore the issue.

With the wheat comes the chaff. "Spirituality" is a popular word of diffuse meaning, and it often seems to mean little more than "using imagination to feel good." But much of what is being written is worth exploring.

Two Guidelines for Making Applications

I have come to use two principles to guide me in selecting sermon illustrations that connect faith with work. First, it is important that any illustration not be naive or simplistic. I include myself in the community of pastors who have offered passionate statements about great truths in a way that makes me feel good but might not be of much help to the people listening. In an article in the *Harvard Business Review,* Andrew Stark noted the tendency of ethics professors to assume that everyone else inhabited the same high-and-dry ground of academia, when most people feel they live and work in the much more difficult and swampy lowland of life.[10] It is one thing to affirm that we should love everyone or that God demands justice; it is another to show how to love or to promote justice in a setting that doesn't play by theological rules.

We can see this by looking again at the prodigal son story. How "forgiving" should someone be toward an employee? The issue comes into play often with substance abuse, such as alcoholism. An employee is a hard worker and likable, but he goes on a spree and misses several days of work. He wants to come back and is genuinely "repentant." Should he be accepted back? If we listen to people at work, we can usually hear stories that suggest such forgiveness can be a part of healing and restoring a life. Troubled employees are sometimes able to rebuild their lives, and the risk to forgive bears much fruit for all concerned. But sometimes, ten days later the employee leaves again and the whole company suffers. The decision is made not to rehire the person. Was the first act of forgiveness a mistake—or a "holy" risk worth taking? The truth is, *in the workplace it's a tough call.* It's a risk that might or might not prove worthwhile. Such is the tension in real life. The tension, of course, is also present in the story itself; Jesus doesn't tell us what happens after the father pleads with the older brother to accept his wayward brother.

Diehl describes the difference in a helpful way. He tells a story from the early days of the environmental movement. Denominations and pastors were condemning corporate pollution and called on steel companies such as Diehl's unilaterally to reduce pollution through expensive systems. Diehl knew that his company could not make such a unilateral move and stay in business because the cost of making the improvements would have to be added to the price of the product and would push the price of the steel beyond what the market could bear. Instead, Diehl encouraged his church and denomination to pressure Congress to impose the necessary regulations on the industry as a whole. When this happened, all the manufacturers made the improvements, the price of everyone's steel was higher, and no one was forced out of business for doing the right thing.

A second guideline I have adopted is to use illustrations that are primarily positive in tone, that show how something worthwhile can be done, and not just to condemn the absence of righteousness. When people in my study were asked, *What activities inspire you?* a recurring response was stories of people overcoming odds to accomplish something meaningful. I wondered how often I had told such stories that were set in the workplace. As Diehl notes in his reflections, the rare occasions when he heard business mentioned in sermons, it was usually as an example of greed. He identifies three basic ways that faith can find expression in work: through competence, affirmation, and support. Texts that speak of our call to care for others can suggest how this can be done not only in nursing homes and soup kitchens but also in the workplace.

To be sure, there is ample opportunity to identify the presence of corporate greed, but that can be matched by alternate examples of someone in business overcoming greed. For example, in one month both *Business Week* and *The MacNeil/Lehrer News Hour* featured stories about the newest CEO of a major paper company and how he had devastated the lives of hundreds of employees in a dramatic drive for a better "bottom line." At the same time, ample coverage was given to a factory owner in Massachusetts who kept his employees on the payroll even after a key building burned. In a sermon dealing with the theme of caring for others, I first noted the negative story about what can happen when there is no concern for others, but I followed it with the story of the factory owner.

Positive examples of doing what is right don't have to be about publicly known figures. For example, I told a story about someone in my congregation whose hospital lab had been permeated by a gossipy, complaining atmosphere. This parishioner told how she decided one day she would simply refuse to go along with conversations that were critical of coworkers, not by making a great speech but by simply redirecting the conversation. People at first were surprised that she wasn't joining in, but eventually the negative atmosphere dissipated. A simple, quiet act had tangible results.

Trying to be positive is not meant to soften the prophetic call of the faith. There are times in a community when the best choice is to take an Amos-like stand against economic injustice or to challenge prevailing assumptions about work and rampant materialism. The point is to make a conscious choice, not just an easy or emotional one. And, I suspect, such a prophetic discernment and judgment will be received with much more respect if people, particularly those in business, believe the preacher knows that not all corporate people are villains and that trying to live a moral life in industrial society is not a simple task.

A Word about Liturgy

The forgoing has been focused on preaching, but preaching is not the only event in a worship service. If a congregation has a strong liturgical tradition, preaching might not even be the most important aspect of communication between God and the people. But working issues can be easily integrated into the rest of the service. Litanies can make reference to working situations and concerns. Children's sermons can portray people living out their faith in work situations. Prayers can regularly include petitions for schools, farms, businesses, and all the places people are employed. Work can also be incorporated into the service visually. At my church in Washington, we began having not only flowers on the altar but arrangements of various fruits as they came into blossom and during harvest. Other symbols of work can be placed in conspicuous places to convey the nonverbal message that what happens in worship is a part of, not separate from, everyday life. The point is a simple one: If we are mindful of the opportunities for integrating work issues into congregational life, much can be done.

Back to the Pew

So imagine again being that person in the pew. You hear the text read. You hear it interpreted within its biblical context and some words about what it means. Your heart stirs as you seem to draw close not just to the meaning of the text but more importantly to the heart of God. You then hear a story about how it is embodied in your personal relationship with God, followed by a story about how it relates to the activities of your church. But then you hear one more illustration expressing the theme— and this one has to do with your workplace. At first you are surprised to hear a story that is set in a company like your own. But as you hear the story, it begins to illuminate the way you experience work—the tensions, the ambiguities, the hopes. And you are led by the story to see a way

God became present in a situation just like yours. It didn't make everything easy or pure, but suddenly you think, to paraphrase Jacob at Bethel,
"Maybe God is in this (work)place, and I didn't know it." The service
ends, and you move into the rest of your Sunday.

On Monday morning you return to work. You go through the mo-
tions and routines. In many ways, this world is very different from the
one where you were the previous morning. But it doesn't really seem like
you're living in two worlds. It's one world. You have an idea how what
you heard Sunday morning might help you handle the challenges you're
facing in the week. And it's good to know that, no matter where you are,
you're not completely on your own. The work of your hands is meant to
flow out of the work of your heart.

Roses bloom and fade. Good mulch lives.

CHAPTER 4

At Coffee Hour and in the Office: The Work of Pastoral Care and Spiritual Direction

Linda's Dilemma

Linda was unhappy and nothing seemed to help. She was irritable, often getting into fierce arguments with her teenage daughter. She had seen her physician. She and her husband had tried counseling. They had prayed for God to lift her spirits. They had gone to a Marriage Encounter weekend, which several years earlier had renewed their relationship. Nothing seemed to help. Her husband confided to me how stressful their life had become. It seemed to be an insoluble situation.

One day Linda's husband dropped by my office to tell me her depression was dissipating. She was starting to laugh again. The arguments with her daughter were becoming less frequent. They were feeling the tension in their relationship ease. When I asked what had made a difference, he told me: She had a new job. Her old job was at a preschool where she had been an aide. For several years she had enjoyed the position. But she had been given little responsibility, and it no longer provided satisfaction. She had found a new job at a drug store in the center of town, and she was now seeing friends and acquaintances throughout the day. She was in charge of a department and was invigorated by the responsibility. In short, the change in work had done what prayer, counseling, and her doctor could not do: give her a rewarding and meaningful activity.

Linda's story has come to my mind often as I have reflected on the ways we can care for one another in Christian community. In seminary, I was trained to anticipate a variety of issues that can affect people: grief, family and marital stress, ethical dilemmas, physical illness, existential faith questions. But I had never been trained to look for how work can effect our health and wholeness. Work was a kind of diagnostic blind spot. Linda's situation was my wake-up call. In the last several years, as I have become attuned to work in people's lives, I have been surprised how often it appears as a significant issue for people. It becomes problematic in different ways.

Bread on the Table

One of the most basic aspects of work is the simple but fundamental truth that our work is usually what provides us with the basic necessities of life. Life—from one-celled organisms to maple trees to human beings—requires effort. Even the monastic traditions whose members took a vow of poverty and begged for life's necessities relied on *somebody's* work—of growing, harvesting, and milling wheat in order to make a loaf of bread, or of spinning wool into thread and weaving cloth to make a tunic. At times, of course, our culture can hide the work behind the goods. We can live our whole life eating carrots from plastic bags and never see the ground they come from. We can spend time in school or on vacations in which we aren't "working" and still eat. But common sense tells us that food, shelter, health care, and education, not to mention the arts, recreation, and entertainment, can exist only with human labor.

Of course, modern American society has far exceeded a basic standard of living. We expect a great abundance of foods and things. We don't need all of that, but we do need some of it. And to obtain it, we need to work.

Although this might seem obvious, it is important to recognize this issue in pastoral care. When someone loses a job or faces the prospect of losing a job, the fear is not just an emotion to be managed. It can be an appropriate emotion that signifies the magnitude of the loss of a home, a place in the community, stability.

At times, I have not quite grasped this. I have had the odd habit of assuming that all human problems could be solved with the right attitude and a dash of spirituality.

Four years after seminary, I left a secure staff position to be a volunteer in mission at an apple farm and retreat center. In exchange for work, my wife and I received housing, some food, and two hundred

dollars per month. At first this was an exciting time. Freed from the re-
straints of parish schedules, I had much more time to pursue my personal
interests. But after a few months, it became clear that we would need
more than two hundred dollars to meet some of our needs. I began apply-
ing for various jobs. I did not get hired. Weeks went by, and winter set
in. We had used up our savings and things were getting tight. One day, it
became clear that our eight-year-old daughter needed to see a dentist. I
took her to a local dentist and got a bill for seventy dollars. When we got
home, it occurred to me that I had no idea where we would get the money.
Suddenly, the basic power of work—its role in putting bread on the
table—became clear to me. No matter what theological understanding I
might choose, the fact was that I needed seventy dollars for my daughter's
health. It was a sobering moment.

This basic fact, that work provides us with necessities, is not star-
tling news to most people in the world, but it can be for theologians.
Adam's original assignment was to till the garden from which food
would come. Such tilling—in whatever form—needs to take place if life
is to exist. It is nonnegotiable. When we listen to people who face situations in which this basic element is being threatened, it is wise to take
the difficulty seriously. Although it might be crucial that people of faith
help others frame such issues in a spiritual context, it is also important to
realize faith communities need to give consideration to the nitty-gritty
issue of getting bread on the table.

The Face in the Mirror

Work not only provides us with life's necessities, it also can be a key
source of our sense of worth. To be needed, to be productive, to be challenged, to accomplish goals, to put bread on the table—all of these things
can give us great satisfaction.

This was certainly the issue for Linda. The job that had once been
enjoyable had lost its value. A change in work that put her in a position
she enjoyed had a positive effect not only on her personally but on her
whole family system. When we feel good about our job, we tend to like
what we see in the mirror.

This issue clearly cuts deep in the psyche of many males. As various writers in gender psychology have noted in recent years, putting

bread on the table is a central source of identity for many males. When I realized I did not have the seventy dollars for my daughter's dentist bill, it wasn't just a practical question: "Let's see, Lord, where will I get the money?" Instead, a deep and primitive voice seemed to be saying to me, "What kind of a man and father are you that you are not providing for your family?"

The issue has been a growing issue for many women. Many working mothers are caught between the desire to be a mother and the desire to have a career. And I have had more than one pastoral conversation with women of a previous generation who spent their lives being supportive of their husbands' careers but in retirement wondered if they were denied an opportunity to pursue and develop a vocation outside of the family.

This sense of worth we derive from work is often cited by anyone who works with the poor and unemployed. Seeing yourself as a failure in the role of breadwinner can unleash all kinds of negative thoughts and lead to depression and abuse. It's potent stuff. When we perceive ourselves to be failing in this regard, it's hard to want to look in the mirror at all.

People can go the other way as well. A common issue in marital problems is the husband's attitude toward work. Work for many men can become all consuming. They spend so much time hunting bears that they are never home participating in the life of the hearth. As one parishioner told me as she described her concern for an estranged son-in-law, "The problem is that he has the wrong God. He worships money."

From a spiritual and pastoral point of view, what do we say? Surely it is appropriate to help one another stay grounded in the truth that we are beloved children of God, whether we are employed or not. Jesus chose the lifestyle of an itinerant, unemployed person and had his needs met. But that level of spiritual trust and maturity is not easy to achieve or maintain, particularly with a family to care for. The need to provide is a deep and tangible one.

I have wondered at times if we don't all live somewhere along a continuum between Donald Trump and Mother Theresa. At the Trump end of the spectrum is the attitude that we cannot rest until we have gained every material advantage possible. At the Mother Theresa end is the way of voluntary poverty, trust that God will provide every true need. At stages in my life, I have aspired to live closer to Mother Theresa's end of the continuum. By doing so, I have found some wonderful blessings. But I have also known some traumatic and tense times that I don't want to revisit unnecessarily. I move back and forth on this continuum, trying to be both faithful and wise.

When caring for each other, the significance of the issue of work as a source of self-respect needs to be recognized. It can be a healthy expression of our Creator's intent, or it can become a powerful force that can wreak destruction. The question "How is work going?" can lead to trivial small talk. Or it can lead to moving expressions of pain, anger, fear, frustration—or joy and satisfaction. We would be wise to listen carefully for the response.

Work and Physical Health

We also need to recognize the importance of work for people's physical health. Work can be a positive factor in health. We all know how good it feels to be involved in work we enjoy. The word "feels" designates more than just an emotion—we literally *are* in better physical health when we enjoy our work. We tend to sleep well, take care of ourselves, and find it easier to have a positive attitude toward life in general.

This is true no matter what occupation people are engaged in. Even the volunteer work people do for a church can impact the health and lives of individuals. Each church I have served has had at least one or two congregational handymen who show up regularly to fix and maintain the church. Often, the spouse will at some point confide to me that such work gives these men a great sense of satisfaction and meaning. One of these men told me that he knew he had literally lived longer because of the exercise and satisfaction he received from caring for the church grounds. I've heard other affirmations of the therapeutic role that church work can play. People who have jobs that aren't totally fulfilling often say volunteer service in a church as a choir member, board member, or teacher gives them a deep sense of satisfaction that contributes to health.

On the other hand, we know well that work can be a contributing factor in illness. One couple's story is typical. Following retirement from an aeronautical firm, they had bought an avocado farm. Managing the farm in the midst of floods, blights, and the fluctuating market turned out to be a relentless source of worry. Finally, they sold the farm and moved into town. On a recent visit to his cardiologist, the man was told that the cardiac concerns they had been tracking seemed to have disappeared. He not only felt better, his heart was *literally* healthier. As has been documented in recent years, work-related stress is an oft-cited cause of a wide range of health problems. Burnout can create physical problems not only for anxious farmers, but also for mothers of young children, engineers holding on to jobs in downsizing companies, and well-meaning pastors.

It can be helpful when we are trying to understand someone's illness to consider the role work might play. When someone is physically ailing, it might be simply the result of a virus or any number of diseases. But it also might have some connection with work. As we listen to each other, it might be worth asking: Are there ways you could become healthier that have nothing to do with medications? Are you overworked? Is it time for you to explore changing jobs? Or are you underworked; do you need to find something tangible to give you purpose and opportunity? By exploring such issues, we can help one another recognize options we need to consider if we are to regain health.

Work and Marriage

The issues already discussed in this chapter often turn up in the form of marital conflict. The spouse who works too much or who is out of work, the parent who feels he or she is not providing for a family, someone who goes every day to a job that has lost its meaning—all of these issues affect not only the individual involved but the spouse and other family members, as well.

I continue to be surprised by how often issues of work contribute to marital conflict. One mother recently shared with me concerns for a daughter who runs a small business with her husband. They spend twenty-four hours a day together and have lost a sense of their relationship apart from their business. Another couple, having managed to bring a business through difficult times, has been overwhelmed by the stress. A young couple in premarital counseling is faced with the issue of each finding work they enjoy in the same town. Until they work this issue through, they have to delay starting a new life together.

The significance here is that the bad feelings about work can easily be transferred and projected onto the spouse or family. It is, of course, the old image of the supervisor mistreating the employee, who is disrespectful to the spouse, who yells at the kids, one of whom ends up kicking the dog. In such a case, the presenting issue might be the family tension. But the root cause might be the work situation. Identifying the source of the difficulty and reframing the problem as not a family problem alone but a work problem can be a fruitful path that takes the pressure off everyone else, including the confused family dog.

Working for the Greater Good

An important element of our work is the effect is has on the world as a whole. Our work might put bread on the table and give us personal satisfaction, but what effect is it having beyond our personal lives? What is it contributing to God's world?

Some professions are generally recognized as having clear social value. Those in medicine, education, and social service are often drawn into those professions by a sense of higher good. Teachers, doctors, nurses, and social workers might struggle to fulfill all the hopes that led them into their profession, but the social utility of what they do is well established. In a faith community, such work often provides numerous examples of how Christian values can be expressed in the workplace. It is important in conversation to affirm the spiritual values that are clearly at the heart of this work.

Other kinds of work, however, can also provide opportunity to care for and serve others. One woman in my church loves her work as a small business loan officer for a local bank. She knows she can use her skill and training to help make people's dreams come true. Another woman works in a trust department. Many elderly people come to her bewildered by their financial situation. She is able to put them at ease and help them put things in order. Daniel Golman begins his book *Emotional Intelligence* with a story of a bus driver in New York who, on a particularly hot and humid day, was able to transform the passengers mood from sullen to relaxed through his attitude and conversation.[11] Virtually any job involving the public can provide opportunities to show care and compassion and to give meaning. Working in a bank or trust department and driving a bus can be "value-added" occupations to which an individual can bring gifts of care and affirmation that bless people in unexpected ways.

Issues of meaning and social worth come into play in other organizations. The community I now live in has a number of high-tech firms, many of which have done government work, including defense contracting. Those in the defense industry who also take faith seriously often reflect on what they do. They assume some people support their work, while others question it. It's an issue they all think about. At times they feel their work has meaning, and at times they do not. For example, one engineer who has worked for the same company for forty years recently gave a presentation to one of our church groups about his involvement in the Apollo program, with particular attention to his participation in the high drama of Apollo 13. Toward the end of his presentation, he touched on the fact that being involved with such a large group of dedicated people for a peaceful purpose was the highlight of his forty-year career. To use his skill and labor as part of a vast team of people who were united for a common purpose was a thrilling thing.

But such high-profile projects that give people a great sense of meaning are not always common in technological companies. One engineer from the same firm told me that he had enjoyed the challenge and teamwork involved in his labor. Knowing, however, that the final product was a missile that was simply gathering dust in a Saudi Arabian hangar sapped his desire to continue in that career. He felt satisfaction in getting the work done well, and some deep anxiety about the ultimate results of his work.

From a spiritual perspective, our work is meant to bless—to benefit not only ourselves but our community and God's world. Some work clearly does that. Other kinds of work might not benefit society directly, but we can bring an extra element of care or compassion to the job that will open an opportunity for such service. In still other positions, the question of the ultimate value of the work might be more difficult to address. A supportive community of faith should be a place to explore these questions.

When Do I Support and When Do I Challenge?

An issue that arises in pastoral care, like preaching, is knowing when to be supportive and when to be confrontational. If someone is sharing the stress they are experiencing from working large amounts of overtime, should I simply be a caring presence and help them return to the fray? Or should I raise the question, "Is it time to look for a new job?" If someone is wrestling with an ethical question at work, God might not want me to help smooth the wrinkles out but instead to confront the powers involved. Again, it is a complex issue that we need to be willing to explore with people.

Spiritual Direction

Some vocational issues can be resolved through counseling. Sometimes, however, the situation requires spiritual direction. Counseling involves the counselor and counselee in a two-way conversation regarding the person's life that might make reference to God. The desired outcome is some resolution regarding the issues involved. In spiritual direction, a *three*-way conversation involves the director, the directee, and God (the Holy Spirit). In spiritual direction, the process is meant to lead not only to the resolution of an issue but also a deepening and strengthening of the relationship with God. The outcome is not just a problem solved but a spiritual relationship made more intimate.

Spiritual direction does not always involve issues of work. The key issue might be the sense of God's absence brought about by grief. It might be a young person's thirst for God's presence. If the person is retired, the question might be, "What does God want me to do with my life?" But for any one working person who seeks to deepen his or her relationship with God, the issue of work can be important.

If we are acting in the role of spiritual director, we will tend to help people listen for the direction in which we believe God is calling them. It is here that our theological beliefs regarding work might come into play. If we don't believe a person's work has much spiritual importance, we might tend to miss God's leadings in that direction. If, however, we believe spiritual maturity involves the integration of every aspect of life, then questions of occupation and vocation are relevant. The Holy Spirit is far more creative and imaginative than any of us will ever be; surely the Spirit is interested in how our work relates to our relationship with God.

Take someone like Roger. Roger and his wife came to my church initially to have a new child baptized. Gradually he began to be more

involved in church. First, he regularly attended worship. Then he became
active in a Bible study. When Roger was a teenager, God had been more
a distant concept than a personal reality, but Roger was now seeking God
with a great earnestness and hunger. And as his involvement in church
and efforts to become closer to God increased, our conversations went
from friendship to informal counseling to spiritual direction. The searching became more acute when Roger decided to leave a career he had
been involved in for many years. The job put bread on the table but did
not give him a sense of worth or value. He wanted to find his "vocation"
—something that would help provide for his family but that he also enjoyed, and something that would also be of service to people. Along with
the basic questions of faith, (How do we find God? Why is there pain
and suffering? Who is Jesus?) came the questions: What does God want
me to do with my career? And how can I know that?

As Roger and I have worked through this time in his life, it has
been, like so many spiritual journeys, a mixture of joy and frustration.
But we are working on the assumption that the Holy Spirit is active in his
life, wanting him not only to find a closer relationship with God but also
to find work that reflects who he is and what God needs in the world.
The question about work has become fertile ground for seeking God's
wisdom and presence. The goal is not just for him to find the right vocation, but for him *to be guided by God* to it and so to find something
profound.

Spiritual direction can involve work issues in other ways. One person in my present church has always had a strong faith and been a loyal
member of the congregation. For several years, he held a position as a
supervisor in a large engineering firm that was undergoing major downsizing, requiring employees to work sixty to seventy hours a week. During this time, the best he could do in church was to be present physically.
Finally he accepted an early retirement offer. In the year and a half since
retirement, he has become a new person. He has become passionately
involved in his own spiritual formation and has begun to play a role in
our congregation's growth in this area. When I have talked to him about
this transformation, he has said that work had put him in a survival mode
in which it was almost impossible for him to be genuinely open to God.
Now that he has the time to do so, his greatest joy is finding opportunities to be open. The point here is that work can so dominate our psyches
that it might be impossible for us to find God in a meaningful way. Once

the stress of a job is removed, suddenly our soul comes alive. Such times are rich times for spiritual direction.

A Simple Lesson

Work is one aspect of wholeness. Our sense of self, our physical well-being, our relationships with other people and with God, and our work are all elements of personal wholeness. By definition, when all parts of this life system are functioning well, the entire system, the person, is whole. When one part is damaged in any way, when it is no longer *in itself* whole, the entire system lacks wholeness. And when one element changes—positively or negatively—the other elements are affected. Hearts and hands are part of one body.

Work is "whole" when it meets basic economic needs, provides for personal satisfaction and meaning, and is recognized as benefiting the world. When work is whole, it can have a positive effect on our psychological, physical, relational, and spiritual life. When work is damaged or incomplete in some way, we will no longer enjoy personal wholeness.

There seemed to be no solution to Linda's irritability with her daughter, her strained marriage, and her depression. As it turned out, a change in one aspect of Linda's life—her work—was the key to her healing. Whether as pastoral counselors or spiritual directors, or simply as Christian brothers and sisters, we can contribute to another's wholeness. Psychological, physical, relational, and even spiritual needs are often obvious, and we easily remember to check for damage in those areas when we talk with someone who is in pain. The wise pastor or friend also remembers to inquire about a hurting person's work. In our work we might find great brokenness—and great opportunity.

CHAPTER 5

In Classrooms and on Retreats: The Work of Education

The Third Line on the Newsprint

It was at one of our adult spiritual formation retreats that you could see the issue plainly. Given the task of portraying his life story with newsprint and colored markers, one participant had drawn a curving path that began at birth and turned and twisted across the page covering events over a fifty-year period. What was significant about this particular timeline was that the person had drawn three paths using three different colors. He explained that one color represented his spiritual search, one his love for music, and the third his work. As he put it, it has not been difficult to blend music and faith—those two colors were often close to each other. But work has been a little more challenging. The colored line representing work came to an abrupt end in his drawing; it was the one line of his life that was yet to be blended with the others. There was a pause. Everyone in the circle understood.

The process of spiritual maturation is one of integration. God is bigger than any job, profession, or economy. But if God can count every hair on our head, then God certainly is present when we are waiting at the copy machine, having a conversation in the teacher's lounge, or listening to a customer's concerns. Education in a congregation offers a unique opportunity for integrating all aspects of our lives, including work. Like other aspects of church life, education has the potential for bringing the lines of our life together.

This, of course, is not always recognized either by those who plan education or those who participate. In most congregations, it is easy to go through a year of educational programs, classes, and events and make no conscious connection with issues of work. But such programs do not adequately serve the people who make up our faith communities. God sees our lives—and all of life—in terms of wholes. Our spiritual lives do not consist merely of time spent in prayer or worship, or at the church for a meeting. A "spiritual life" is one in which God's presence, guidance, and glory are sought in every aspect of what we do. The movement of God's Spirit is meant to flow through our hearts to find expression in the work of our hands. Educational activities can lead to a greater sense of wholeness when work is routinely recognized as an integral part of who we are.

Adult Education

Adult education programs provide a ready-made setting for examining work issues. In the church I am serving now, we developed a simple, four-week series on spirituality and work. In the first session, I offered scriptural and theological background on the general topic of faith and work. We then had different lay people speak about what it is like for them to try to integrate their faith and occupation. One research scientist described how he balances the disciplines of the scientific method, in which one needs to be always skeptical, with faith, in which genuine questioning blends with trust and belief. Another scientist offered a compelling vision of how God is revealed for him in the natural world. Another Sunday, people from higher education described how they have found ways to embody their faith in a secular institution that inhibits religious expression. Such a series has the advantage of giving a congregation—and pastor—the opportunity to look over the shoulder of people working at integrating faith and work.

Our congregation is creating a new series, "Making a Life While Making a Living." This series has developed over a period of time as I have listened to the recurring issues expressed by people trying to make sense of work, career, and faith. It is designed to offer participants information from different disciplines that all impact vocation, occupation, and competency in contemporary economic society. We will begin with a session on theological assumptions regarding work and stewardship, both from our own biblical heritage and other religious traditions. We will hear a presentation from a career counselor on finding or changing careers. A marriage and family counselor will share insights regarding the way work impacts people and families. A personal financial consultant will discuss common questions about money management and financial planning. Throughout the series, there will be time not only for discussion but also practical exercises that will enable people to make immediate application of what has been discussed.

Other models are readily available. Many denominations have developed study papers, theological statements, and curricula about work. A topical Bible study can be created to examine the role of work in various biblical stories and personalities. Reading groups can be formed to discuss books such as William Diehl's *The Monday Connection* or works by people such as Covey, Greenleaf, and Senge. Professionals from the community can be invited to offer their perspective. In short, adult education offers a variety of ways to help people begin to integrate their faith and work.

Small Group Ministry

Small groups, a mainstay of many healthy churches, are also natural settings in which congregations can address work issues. Diehl describes how to design and support small groups that focus on work issues. In one model, people from diverse professions gather once a month for breakfast. At each session, someone presents a challenging situation they are facing at work. The group discusses options that are both consistent with Christian faith and pragmatic. Pastors act as resource support persons in such groups, not as experts or leaders. At the end of each session, someone else volunteers to be the presenter.

Small groups don't have to deal intentionally with work issues to be significant in peoples' progress towards integration. In our congregation, anywhere from three to ten small groups meet, depending on the time of year. Given an opportunity to discuss important situations in their lives, many people will invariably offer work situations. Affirmation, listening, discussion, and prayer help strengthen them and give them guidance. Some members of such groups have said that the support of the group has been the most important factor in helping them keep a sense of integrity and meaning at work

Retreats

Retreats offer another method for promoting the integration of faith and work. While retreats will often be built around particular speakers or themes that might not have direct impact on work issues, often there are times when work can and should play a role.

One option is to have a retreat specifically focused on the issue of spirituality and work. Formats for such retreats can vary. One model for such a retreat, *Linking Faith and Daily Life*, has been developed through the Episcopal church. The product of a three-year study and experiment, the program is designed to help working people reflect on the role work plays in their faith journeys.

But working issues need not be at the center of a program; they can be addressed in other ways. At my current church, we have developed a simple weekend adult spiritual retreat program called "Crossroads" that we offer twice a year. We begin with a Friday night dinner and fellowship time. On Saturday morning we have a Bible study on the chosen text for the weekend. Participants then do an activity that lets them use the text as a way to interpret their life's journey. Later in the day, we tell these stories and move into activities that include prayer and celebration. Sunday morning we have several closing activities. Anyone who has worked with spiritual retreats knows that a recurring challenge is to connect the "mountain-top experiences" from the retreat with the less-protected lives we all live when we return. To that end, we always include a Sunday-morning activity in which participants are asked to describe a difficult situation they are facing in their personal lives or at work. Each person is then asked, How can what you have learned at the retreat make a difference in that situation? The responses become part of our closing time. Work issues often surface. We might hear about a possible promotion, the effects of possible downsizing, or a difficult supervisor or coworker. Of course, the described issue might not be about work. But my experience is that anywhere from one-third to one-half of the retreatants describe a work situation.

The point here is that work is not a primary focus of these retreats; the focus is on encountering God through Scripture and life experiences. But we give permission to let the issue of work surface. From a leader's point of view, this takes no additional preparation, only simple mindfulness. In this way, work issues arise as a natural outgrowth of a desire for deeper communion with God. Spirituality can become truly integrative.

Work issues can also be incorporated in retreats that feature psychological and spiritual profiles. The Myers-Briggs Type Indicator, for example, illuminates relational issues and prayer styles, and is also useful in understanding relationships in the workplace. Similarly, work with the enneagram can offer insight into working situations. Making these connections not only offers important information but models an understanding of spirituality that integrates all the major aspects of our lives.

Ministry through Families and with Youth

A healthy church prepares youth for the real world. This involves equipping youth by helping them become familiar with Scripture, church teaching and traditions, life in community, and service. But you also need to be prepared for the realities of work. If we do not help prepare them, we not only fail to help them with some of the most crucial decisions they will make; we have also conveyed the message that the church is more interested in itself than in the people who attend.

As every educator knows, children learn not just what they are taught in classrooms but what they observe in their interaction with adults. Worship is a place where young people form an image of what is *really* important to the church (and, by implication, to God). Liturgy, children's sermons, and adult sermons that never make reference to work and secular life will build an image of faith as something separate from everything else. Learning for youth will begin with what they see adults talk about, act on, and celebrate. A church that regularly refers to work issues will show youth that faith has relevance for all of life.

Youth also learn from the modeling they see in their own families. The values absorbed in childhood, for example, can guide an adult in the workplace years later. In my research project, I was surprised how often these adult leaders looked back to the spiritual dimension of their youth. Donna Anderson, president of the National Retiree Volunteer Coalition, said:

I was brought up in a German, Lutheran family. I thought everyone was taught to work hard, to respect others, to give of yourself to those around you, to keep your room clean and make your bed before you leave the house.

Another respondent, Kent Skipper, noted:

> I was raised in a mainstream Protestant faith by parents who viewed
> their faith as central to their lives and who attempted to live by those
> precepts daily. They worked hard to teach me and demonstrate by
> example that our purpose in life is caring, sharing, and helping.
> Their insistence on tolerance, even of the intolerant, and empathy
> for those less fortunate than ourselves were powerful influences in
> my life. They were joyful, exciting people who never acted piously
> or demonstrated self-satisfaction. These experiences in my family of
> origin had a profound effect on my values and beliefs.

Similar themes were evident in the reflections of one public official who
wrote:

> I became a Catholic because at a stage in my life when I was too
> young to understand, my mother and father took me to church and
> had a priest pour holy water on my head and say words in Latin.
> Eventually, my religion—and its traditional beliefs—became a mat-
> ter of conviction. Those traditions, while recognizing that we are too
> weak to do it perfectly, call on us nevertheless to try to do good
> things for other people.

Such comments are important in that they remind us of the important ways in which spiritual education takes place in the lives of many
children through a family's expression of its spirituality. Such lessons
can have enormous impact in workplaces decades later. Ministry to and
through families is a crucial aspect of a church's mission to people who
will work in secular organizations.

In addition to working through worship and family life, educating
youth for an integrated life can take place in more formal and intentional
ways. Opportunities include the following:

• As children begin to reach junior high age, for a few sessions each year
invite adults to come as guest speakers to Sunday school or youth group
meetings to talk about work and faith.

• If a church has a confirmation program, one part of the curriculum can explore faith and work. In our congregation, we require each student to meet with at least two people to discuss how to view work from a faith perspective. The student can then either write a short summary of what they learned or simply convey that in class discussion.

• As young people reach high school age, the issue of career begins to loom larger. Discussions about work and money can be included with topics such as morality, dating, and marriage. Adults who can establish rapport with teenagers can be invited to lead discussions about how someone might begin to prepare for an occupation that can also be a vocation. A more ambitious program can emulate what many public high schools do: place students for a day or week with a mentor in a profession of the student's choice. This "real life experience" can stimulate reflection and discussion about the student's aspirations and the realities of society.

In a church where any or all of these possibilities are pursued, there is a good chance that young people will gain some bit of information or wisdom that will impact their life choices. But just as important, if not more so, the young person will learn the *implicit* lesson that work and spirituality are not two separate realities but part of a whole. That is the way God sees our lives, and that is the way we are meant to live.

Seeing the Third Line in a New Way

The person at the retreat who drew his three life lines described his desire that all three lines come together, that the work line not be separate from the other two. He went on to describe a recent conversation with a spiritual director in which he was laying out this hope for integration. The conversation was taking place outside a monastery, which had an impressive view of the valley below. He became aware of how much could be seen from this vantage point and found himself seeing all the aspects of his life as more connected than he had assumed. Work already *was* a part of his whole life. All three lines *did*—together—represent his life. Everything in his life was summarized on that one piece of newsprint. As he described this insight at the retreat, he opened us all to the possibility of seeing that from a broad perspective, our lives are indeed integrated.

If people are searching for integrated lives, we need to help in that search. We need to do it not only in worship and in private conversations, but also in classrooms, through programs, and on retreats. There, in a group of peers, we find a time and place to try to make connections between the different aspects of our lives and to make room for the Holy Spirit. The Spirit is waiting to help us, always ready to work.

CHAPTER 6

At the Monthly Meeting: The Work of Leadership

In every church I have served, there was a place I could go to get a panoramic view of the community I worked in. In my current congregation, that place is appropriately called "Inspiration Point." Getting to Inspiration Point requires a fifteen–minute drive followed by a forty-five-minute, uphill hike. As the name implies, the effort is well worth it. From Inspiration Point I can see the whole area along the Pacific Coast that constitutes my community. The roof line of my church building is not visible, but I know where the church is. At times, during a worship service or a board meeting, when something significant happens, I can almost believe that the church is the center of the community, or even the world. But I know that is not true because from Inspiration Point I can plainly see all the other places that make up our community: the university, the neighborhoods, the airport, the schools, the businesses. I can also see Highway 101 as it carries traffic in a steady stream, cars and trucks that might be headed just a few miles or all the way to Canada to the north or Mexico to the south. Our church building is a significant place for me, but it is only one building among many others in town, and our congregation is part of something much greater. The question becomes, What are we doing in our church that is making a difference in this community and world? Where are we headed? Where does God want us to be? These are not easy questions, but they are good questions, and they bring up the importance of leadership.

After a career in private enterprise and public service, Robert Greenleaf described the role of churches in developing leadership:

I believe that, in a society in which so much caring for persons is mediated through institutions, the most open course to build a more

just and caring society is to raise the performance as servants of as
many institutions as possible by new regenerative forces initiated
within them by committed individuals: servants. And who will
nurture the servants who make this commitment? I believe it will be
the churches that are inspired and guided by spirituality as leadership that emerges from contemplation and theological reflection.12

Greenleaf's challenge is clear: the church needs to take a leadership role
in the development of leaders across society.

Leadership is about many things. It is about seeing wholes. It is
about discerning where we are and imagining where God wants us to be.
It is about seeing how things are connected. It is about relating to ourselves and other people in a way that is congruent with our values. And
it is all about trying to make a difference.

If a congregation is to be the church, it needs to see itself as an inspiring place where people come to reflect on every aspect of their lives
and to practice how they want to live. By doing that faithfully, a congregation is fulfilling its mission. But the value of such a congregation does
not end in itself. *What we do within should always have impact without.*
If a congregation is to serve people who work, it needs to equip them for
leadership and discipleship not just within the congregation but in the
world outside the church walls. Therefore, as we spend time in meetings
making decisions, it is helpful to keep in mind some basic aspects of
leadership and how they can be transferred beyond the church.

Vision

There is a difference between management and leadership. Management
is taking care of things the way they are—maintaining the status quo.
Good management skills are vital to any organization. But management
is not enough to make an organization transformative. Transformative
leadership involves taking care of things, but it also involves being constantly focused on a preferred future. That preferred future is often described as a vision. Leadership means responding to present events with
a larger vision.

The difference between the two can be illustrated from Scripture. In
the Exodus story, the Israelites needed management skills to survive in

Egypt. But to find something better than Egypt, they needed the vision of liberation and a promised land. God gave Moses that vision, Moses communicated it to the people, and their liberation began.

In Jesus' time, people were also faced with the job of managing their situation as best they could. But Jesus came with a vision of something more, another, greater reality known as the kingdom of God. The apostles became leaders when they began to respond to situations with an eye on that greater reality. Every encounter became an opportunity to seek Jesus' kingdom.

One of the simplest ways to be reminded of our vision is to ask the question, What is our higher purpose here? Are we leading worship by rote, or are we planning services with a vision of people encountering the living God? Are we developing a budget to pay bills, or are we developing a budget to accomplish Christ's work in the world? Am I developing my sermon to get pats on the back, or am I trying to communicate the power and closeness of God?

Peter Senge points out that the vision in a healthy organization provides a creative tension, and he maintains that there is a always an optimum tension between vision and reality. It is like stretching a rubber band: If we stretch too far, the rubber band might break; if we stretch it only a little, the rubber band dangles loosely and carries little potential energy. Senge believes that every organization should always be stretching itself between a vision for what it can be and its present reality. It should not have an impossible vision, for then the tension might be too great. But the organization needs to have some vision, or else there is no life in it. Senge also asserts that the best vision does not necessarily come from a solitary person "on high," but can be most effective when developed by a group of people in the organization. He calls this "shared vision."[13]

Whether it comes from one leader, a board, or a whole congregation, vision can be demonstrated in many ways. It is often embodied in a mission statement. It is called on at turning points in congregational life—calling a new pastor, beginning a building program, facing a reduction in program or staff. It should show up in some way in every newsletter. It should be part of every leadership retreat. It's an image, a statement, a creed that answers the question: Why is this church here? What do we think we are trying to do?

The church's vision begins with the profound reality of God and then emerges out of the relationship between that reality and the particular congregation. And by trying to live up to that vision, the church might encourage people to live by such a vision in other organizations.

Few secular organizations will see the kingdom of God as the master metaphor for their organizational vision. Even if the leaders of the organization wanted to focus on the kingdom of God in their vision, it would be difficult to do so in a pluralistic society. But if the church can continually raise up this vision in a compelling way, people at work can claim the kingdom as an *underlying* vision as they operate within their organizations.

One lay person who embodied such a vision worked as a principal in a public high school. It was not one of the easier high schools to administer because it was situated in a poor area that was prone to ethnic conflict. But this man worked tirelessly in his job. His values were his driving force, but he never forced them on anyone else. He treated all students and faculty with dignity, even when he didn't agree with them. He withstood criticism with grace. Knowing him as I did, I was aware stress and tension could accumulate for him. But when I listened to him reflect on his life, it was clear that what gave his work integrity was that he held up the Gospel's vision for humanity as the vision for his work.

Another person who is attempting to live out the vision of the Gospel in his work is Tom Chappell, CEO of Tom's of Maine. In his life story, *The Soul of a Business*, Chappell describes his journey from corporate success story to depressed midlife seeker to seminary student to renewed leader. He now tries to hold up the biblical vision of humanity become the vision for his company. For instance, instead of seeing his employees as boxes on an organizational chart, he draws on Paul's image of the interdependent body in 1 Corinthians 12. Each employee has a different function, but all are essential to the health of the body. Trying to live out this vision is not easy; Chappell is clear that he does not find it possible, for example, to let the "whole body" make every decision by consensus to strive to make every corporate move be popular. But the vision continues to be a guiding force.

Another person who has sought to let the biblical vision be a guiding one in work is Max DePree. DePree is an active church member as well as CEO of Herman Miller Furniture in Michigan. Depree sees the purpose of his organization as making a profit—and more. Describing his practice of making clear the underlying premises in his organization, he states:

...what we believe preceded policy and practices. Here I am talking about both our corporate and personal value systems. It seems to me that our value system and world view should be as closely integrated into our work lives as they are integrated into our lives with our families, our churches, and our other activities and groups....[14]

In a compelling vision, all elements of our pluralistic society are taken into account. It might not be appropriate for a secular organization to convey a vision that uses specific theological language or images. But the *underlying* vision and assumptions of our faith can help form our visions.

The vision of the kingdom of God is proclaimed in the church but is not to be contained within it. The vision has no boundaries. It is meant to lead every church—and its people—wherever they are.

Practicing Right Relationship

The church is not just a place where we hold up God's vision. It is a place where we try to put the vision into practice week after week, season after season.

Some years ago I heard the theologian Tom Boyd speak on the term "practicing Christian." He suggested that the term can sometimes be a little intimidating because it suggests we are trying to live up to a standard of flawlessness. But he said the term can instead offer a great deal of freedom. After all, if someone is practicing the piano, we are not surprised if she hits a wrong note or chord. After all, she is not performing, she is "just practicing." We aren't called to flawless performance. But we are called to continuous practicing.

The first element of practice is an openness to having our vision for our life arise out of our relationship with God. Week after week, we practice what it means to be in relationship with God. We listen to God. We pray to God. We fall in love with God. We praise God. We keep practicing what it means to have God rather than ourselves at the center of life. The first aspect of practicing right relationship is to keep practicing fidelity in our relationship to God. In essence, doing this is trying to obey the first of the two great commandments: "You shall love the Lord your God with all your heart, and with all your soul, and with all your mind" (Matt. 22:37).

This right relationship can be expressed in many subtle ways where people work. If people believe God is present every day of the week and every place, then any situation can bring to mind the question of what it means to practice loving God. We can pray for God's guidance as we encounter difficult situations. We can see relationships with others as opportunities for service. We can constantly remember that God is with us.

Trying to practice the first great commandment leads us to the second: "You shall love your neighbor as yourself" (Matt. 22:39). In church, this is what we do when we support one another, care for one another, and practice compassion. We practice loving not only with people we know but with strangers and people in need. Church is clearly one place in society where we are supposed to be practicing loving other people.

At times I have taken this for granted. At other times I have been reminded of this when people have become involved in my church who have lived in highly dysfunctional family systems. One person always comes to mind, a man I will call Bob. Bob started coming to our church almost by accident. By his appearance and manner, it was clear his life had been difficult. He was illiterate and couldn't read the hymn verses or bulletin. When I visited him and heard his life story, he told me about his broken relationships, his scattered family, and how often he'd been in prison. Bob kept coming back week after week to our church. One time he told me why: It was the only place he'd ever been where people treated each other—and him—with respect and kindness. In a sense, he had never had an opportunity to practice basic respect before. The church was the place to do that.

But, again, we practice right relationships in church so that we can practice them in the workplace. The principal mentioned above practiced such relationships continually. He was an ex-Marine and former state champion heavyweight wrestler—an imposing figure. There was a time when tension was running high in the community due to an increase in gangs and drug trafficking. Students were coming onto campus while under the influence of drugs and alcohol. In one such incident, an intoxicated student came onto campus and would not leave. The principal personally asked the student to leave, and the student responded with a physical attack. The principal quickly pinned the student on the ground and held him there until the police arrived. News of this spread through the small town, and people were elated. They said, "One of those kids sure picked the wrong person to tangle with." When I asked the principal about how it felt to be a hero, he told me how discouraged he was by what had happened. He said he continually tells kids that they should not try to settle disputes by physical force. Having resorted to using superior physical force to subdue this student meant he had failed. Although no one questioned what he did, he had such a high standard of living out the Gospel that he felt no pride in defeating the student. But he was going to keep practicing.

People practice right relationships when they find appropriate opportunities to speak out for the kingdom. One of my parishioners told me about having dinner at an affluent retirement home. The table conversation was focused on the question of whether illegal immigrants should receive medical care in California. One of the residents stated clearly that she did not think such people had any right to help at all. The service worker who happened to be clearing the table looked at her, smiled, and said, "You know, we *all* are children of God." We can speak out in such a way even when we are outside the church.

We do not always practice right relationships in the workplace. As we are reminded by the spirituality of Therese of Liseaux, we often practice right relationships in small ways. When people can be coaxed to talk about how they try to live out faith at work, we hear stories about listening with compassion to a coworker who is under stress, forgiving or even loving a supervisor who is overbearing, helping organize an event in the workplace that raises money for a food bank or someone's medical needs. Practicing right relationships is also about not going along with practices that are clearly unethical. It is, in short, all the ways people try to love their neighbor as themselves—to love them because God first loved us.

Church leadership includes holding up God's vision while affirming and encouraging the practice of right relationships, which are the embodiment of that vision. Leaders need to do this in every church. When we lead—when we make decisions and set courses that have an impact on our congregation—the effects of that leadership don't end with the church. The church is but a practice arena for people living and working throughout the community and world.

Valuing Community

One of the key claims of the Gospel is an affirmation of the importance
of community. Jesus didn't chose one or two disciples, he chose twelve.
When he fed the five thousand, he wasn't just feeding individuals, he
was modeling what it means to care for a whole group. When he washed
the disciples' feet, he was acting out what it means to serve one another.
His parables of the kingdom of God often are set in wedding banquets
where a group of people are sharing in the celebration. To be a church is
to practice the reality of the strength of community.

One church I served had an annual turkey dinner. More than 140
volunteers served over 800 people. The tradition began during the depression when the congregation needed money for a building fund. But
in recent years, the amount of money raised was no longer the issue.
People believed in the event and participated in it because it was an annual reenactment of what it means to be a community.

The best moments in a worship service are when the gathered wor-
shippers experience a sense of God's presence. This might be during a
baptism, or when news of someone's need is being laid before the community, or when everyone seems to be singing a hymn with passion.
These are transcendent moments, moments in which the power and
presence of the Holy Spirit are tangible.

Knowing the importance of these experiences, those of us in leadership need to ensure that our congregations experience them. When we
come together for a cause beyond self-interest, we are all made stronger.
That prepares us for other challenges. This emphasis on community is
important, too, for what it can mean for people at work. One of the major
trends in the last five years in business has been a new emphasis on
teams and community. Organizational research has often shown that a
team of people is more creative and effective than a simple collection of
individuals. Peter Senge believes there is a great richness in what he calls
"team learning"—when a group is involved in the process of gaining
new insights, the insights are not only more valuable but the group experiences a deep bonding.[15] Teams are becoming commonplace in many
organizations.

The church can have an impact in this area by being an example of
the power of community. It is a vision that helps a community coalesce.
It is the practice of right relationship that makes a community strong.

Someone nurtured in church community can draw on that experience in the workplace. If we are involved in the leadership of a small business or public agency, the virtues and practices we find at church can help us create community where we work.

But the church also has a special role to play because it can model what it means to be a community or team *apart* from a drive for efficiency or productivity. After all, the reason many organizations use teams is not because of altruism but because of a desire for greater profitability. If some new technique comes along, teams might be displaced by something else. But from a spiritual point of view, the value of community will never be displaced. It is a part of who we are.

In the church, we can take for granted the importance of community. But community should not be taken for granted. Within the church, we should be constantly looking for opportunities to create it, enhance it, and protect it. And we should be aware that the blessings of community are not limited to a congregation. They can extend into the workplace and beyond.

Being Mindful of the Power of Systems

In the great creation images of Scripture, we see that all of life is interrelated. In Genesis, everything develops from God, and everything comes in its place and time. In Psalm 104, we hear praise for God's presence and design in the great array of life. In modern times, we see more evidence of how deeply interrelated all living things truly are. A decrease in Brazilian rain forests means less oxygen in Asia. Industrial emissions in Los Angeles widens a hole in the ozone layer over Antarctica. The decrease in one species causes a ripple effect through other life forms. This interrelationship has become more pronounced on the human, social level as technology and communication have brought cultures closer. Chaos theory tells us that the air wafted by a butterfly's wings in China might eventually create a thunderstorm in New York. We are increasingly aware that we do not exist as independent, self-sufficient organisms but as part of a great, complex web of life.

For Peter Senge, the importance of systems thinking cannot be overemphasized. He identifies systems thinking as one of the hallmarks of any organization that is able to learn from and adapt to change.

Organizations that operate as if they exist independent of other forces are rapidly becoming extinct.

The significance of systems thinking is not difficult to identify in the life of a church. When I was serving as pastor in Washington, there was a national panic over the use of an apple spray known as Alar. This panic led to a sharp decrease in the demand for red delicious apples, which in turn caused a decrease in sales and loss of income for farmers. Farm workers had less work. Owners and workers were not able to give as much to the church as they had in the past. It was not a year when we encouraged members to increase giving. A year later, some of the small farmers I knew were still struggling with despair after taking large losses in the previous year. In short, our ministry was dramatically affected by the use of one agricultural product.

In a different vein, that same church in Washington instituted a comprehensive youth program (the "Logos" program) that requires the involvement of every family in both mid-week activities and Sunday worship. Four years after we began the program, one mother cried as she told a group that this program had not only brought her husband to church but had transformed their family life. All of life is interrelated.

A congregation does not exist in some kind of holy isolation. Population changes, layoffs and hirings, racial tensions, political conflict—all such things affect the people we serve. Many churches have become involved with the homeless, the AIDS epidemic, teenage pregnancy, abortion, and Twelve Step groups in response to changes in society. Similarly, we have seen a decrease in denominational loyalties, Sunday school attendance, and the availability of volunteers due to sociological trends. We exist as one system that is intertwined with many others.

If as leaders we understand and anticipate such changes, we are more in tune with reality and can respond effectively. As Wayne Gretsky, possibly the greatest hockey player of all time, put it, "It's not where the puck is, it's where it's going to be that's important." We anticipate change by keeping an eye on what is happening in our community and world, and we help members prepare for change by talking about it in sermons and newsletters. The leaders of our congregation spend time at retreats or annual meetings reflecting on what will be happening in five, ten, or fifty years and how we can prepare for it. When we study Scripture, we try to imagine not just what it meant in the past but what it will mean in the future.

Anticipating change also helps us be more realistic about what we do. The results of ministry are difficult to measure. As Tom Gillespe, president of Princeton Seminary once said, clergy often get less results than they hope for but do more good than they can imagine. If we remember the truth of systems thinking, it helps us to recognize that something worthwhile we do—a comment in a sermon, the point of a lesson, a decision to encourage someone to take on a leadership position—might have a minimal immediate effect, but a month, a year, or ten years later, it might turn out to have had a significant impact on someone's life.

When we bear in mind the importance of systems thinking, we will model mature spirituality, which recognizes that all of life is part of a great complex of relationships. This modeling can have a genuine impact on people who work.

The truth that all of life is interconnected should underly what is said and done in worship services. The more our worship services include clear, practical application, the more positive the effect they will have. I was preaching a series on First Corinthians and came to the passage in which Paul encourages people not to take every disagreement to civil court. Wanting to offer some guidance for how to avoid ending up in court, we included in the bulletin a summary of the basic steps for conflict resolution set out in the classic work, *Getting to Yes*, with supporting comments from a Christian point of view. Within a few weeks, several people made it a point to say how they were referring to these guidelines as they approached conflict in their workplace and what a difference it was making. Little would Paul have guessed that his response to a problem in Corinth would lead, two thousand years later, to the successful settlement of a dispute in a California workplace.

The ability to integrate spirituality into multiple levels of organizational life is at the heart of true effectiveness. Prominent management consultant and author Peter Vaill describes a significant study about this integration. Vaill believes the dominant reality of modern life is an experience of "permanent white water": so many things are changing so fast that is hard for us to know what we can depend on.

Vaill recently asked a group of thirty-five leaders to describe someone they knew personally who has successfully led an organization through a time of "white water" change. Two characteristics emerged. The first was "the ability to stay with a clear mission and purpose" in the midst of all the confusion. The second was the ability to model "inclusiveness," to keep everyone informed in such a way that they knew they were valuable and being listened to. As Vaill says, this inclusiveness is more than just information. "...It is not an exaggeration in many of the cases to say that the leader expressed love for the members of the system and helped them to love each other."[16] Holding on to a deep vision and being able to love other people—these are aspects of leadership that can originate in our spirituality and radiate in many directions, positively influencing a whole host of interconnected systems.

In my research project, all the leaders involved agreed that spiritual traditions and principles have played a "fundamental" role in the formation of their values. Some are able to express their spirituality in an explicit way. But for the most, being a leader in a secular organization means that spirituality is best expressed in subtle yet personal ways. Bill Schoenhard, executive vice-president of SSM Healthcare System in St. Louis, describes it this way:

> I believe any successful workplace must have a clearly understood mission as well as articulated values which describe the culture of that organization. Obviously, with the exception of a church sponsored organization, these values cannot be ascribed to a particular church or faith tradition. However, I believe that the spiritual values which the leaders or owners of an organization bring to their location should have major influence on the cultural norms by which persons within the organization interact with each other.

Ron Anderson, president and CEO of the Dallas County Hospital District, said:

> I believe that spirituality is a deeply personal issue. You can study religion with some folks and you can pray and worship with others. You can also have very meaningful work relationships without ever getting into ideology or individual philosophy, but certainly by allowing your work mates to express their spirituality in their work product and interaction with other people in the worksite. This really comes down to respect for other persons and love for fellowman. I think this is important in the workplace and it's important in every part of a person's life. I don't think you can have this take the form of organized religion per se, but I think it can emanate from the leadership position and actually fuel relations throughout an organi-

zation simply by setting the tone that expresses an appreciation for others and an awareness of the spiritual aspects of life.

One of the public officials noted the inescapable connection between faith and work:

> Although the American system of government carefully and properly doesn't allow us to impose our religious views on others, as an elected leader you often face what could best be described as spiritual questions: What is our obligation to the poor? to the earth? to the children? to those who have strayed into a life of violence and brutality? Certainly the greatest guide I have in making those decisions is the fundamental spiritual lessons I learned while growing up.

I might think that the fruits of my church's work can only be seen in what happens on Sunday mornings. But if I bear in mind the power of systems, I can lead with a confidence that our influence will be tangible if not always visible. If someone learns in church as a child that all people are to be treated as children of God and that person ends up in a position of influence and power, the effects of that belief can be profound. If someone participates in a church in which humility is practiced as a natural response of faith, that humility exercised in the workplace can enable the person to see reality and possibilities that might not appear to someone else. And, as Robert Greenleaf said, leaders who believe their greatest job is service become very different leaders from those who believe their greatest task is the accumulation of status. The faith community in which these values are modeled might never know what effect it is having, but, from a systems thinking point of view, the effects will be there nevertheless.

We live in a world of interdependent systems. This awareness will make it easier for churches to adapt to change. Leading with this awareness can also have unforeseen effects on people who work.

Another Inspiration Point

Leadership involves many things. In a church, it begins with God at the center. From there it involves, among other things, vision, practicing right relationships, valuing community, and systems thinking. When a church is paying attention to these principles, it will not only be a healthier church but can be a model and inspiration for people to live a more meaningful life where they work.

I was once visiting one of my parishioners in a coronary care unit a few hours before he was to have bypass surgery. I asked how things had been going at work. He had worked for more than twenty-five years in a leadership position in a large, influential public institution that is known as a place of constant conflict and turmoil. He told me about an image that had come to him at a recent worship service. During the sermon, he had found himself looking around the sanctuary at the other people. For a moment he was aware that everyone in that place was practicing being open to God, and he imagined everyone in a circle with God at the center. No one was trying to get in front of anyone else. No one was complaining that they deserved to be in another place. Everyone was content to be just where they were, open and at peace. As he was telling me this, his face was radiant. He and I knew that no organization would ever fully embody that reality. But he and I also knew that this is God's vision for humanity. Having this vision deep within our heart helps us put our workplace in perspective. We can look beyond the frailties of the workplace to see the people and the ways we can try to practice right relationship by serving each other. I don't know what I had been preaching on while he had this vision, but I am he glad he remembered what he saw instead of whatever I had said. Seeing things the way God sees them—that's what counts.

EPILOGUE

The poet and farmer Wendel Berry tells a story about visiting a particular Amish family. He spent several days with them learning how they understood their relationship with the land. At one point, the farmer let Berry see his accounting ledger for the year, the careful record of all his credits and debits. Included in this was an account of how many hours he had worked. Berry said what had surprised him was the column that the farmer had chosen to enter these work numbers: it was on the *credit* side of the ledger. When asked about it, the farmer replied that he considered his labor not an expense that allowed him to get something else, but one of the benefits of being alive. To work on his farm was an opportunity God had given him. Work was a gift.

Such a view of work is hard to find in our society. So many people labor with a sense that work is a curse. "Curse" might express what it is like to labor when our relationship with God is broken. But it is not God's intention. I do not believe Ruth thought it was a curse to glean in the barley fields or David thought it was a curse to be a shepherd. I know Paul did not resent his occupation, nor did Lydia seem to feel a need to turn her back on the textile trade. And my hunch is that when Jesus was fitting an oxen yoke, healing a leper, or composing a story that would challenge the authorities, he did so with a clear sense that work is meant to bless.

But isn't our world a different place? Isn't such integration of work and spirituality possible only in the simpler lifestyles of Galilean peasants and Amish farmers? Is that integration a lost possibility in this confused and high-paced society we live in?

I think not. I believe that living with the guidance of the Holy Spirit will inevitably lead to a spirituality that integrates our work, our relationships, our responsibilities, and our faith. It might be that we cannot live in an integrated manner in some situations or in some organizations. To find such integration we might have to let go of things that seem dear. But I do know people who live such an integrated life. These teachers, farmers, business people, homemakers, elected officials, and engineers wouldn't make such a claim themselves, but their lives exemplify such integration. It is possible.

So which is the real world: the world of work or the world of faith? For many years I thought the answer had to be one or the other. But now I believe both are real. As Parker Palmer has said, spirituality strives "to penetrate the illusions of the external world and name its underlying truth —what it is, how it emerges, and how we relate to it."[17] The spiritual quest does not mean that the "external world" is not real or without value; instead it allows us to see our proper relationship with it. Our task as leaders of congregations is to work with each other to penetrate the illusions, uncover the presence of the living God, and live together in response to grace. We must help each other make the connection between the worship of our hearts and the work of our hands. That is our work, and it is holy work to do.

Twenty-Five Ways to Serve People Who Work

1. Assume God cares about what people do for a living.
2. Assume people care about what they do for a living.
3. Notice how you think and feel about your job.
4. Believe God is at work outside the church walls.
5. Believe God is at work even when no church official is aware of it.
6. Believe God calls us all to lives of meaning.
7. Ask others how they experience work.
8. Know that supporting work doesn't mean supporting dysfunctional or unethical practices.
9. Talk about work in sermons and homilies.
10. Mention people working in children's sermons.
11. Include work issues in prayers.
12. Don't stand on moral high ground unless you know what it's like to live in the swamp.
13. Look for ways work issues might contribute to personal, marital, or family problems.
14. Be aware of work issues when you are acting as a spiritual director.
15. Visit others where they work.
16. Plan adult education series on work, vocation, money management, and career planning.
17. Cultivate a vision for the future based in the reality of God and a clear-sighted understanding of both the present and the future.
18. Believe that good things that happen in church might have effects you will never know about (the butterfly effect).
19. Look for connections in everything.
20. Build community constantly.
21. Recognize that young people need help seeing God's presence in

work and spiritual perspectives on choosing a vocation.

22. Know that we all come to church in part to find a sanctuary from the stresses and challenges of work; create a sanctuary, but also prepare each other for the real tasks we have ahead of us.

23. Practice right relationships in church and at work.

24. Assume life is meant to be lived with God at the center.

25. Believe that work is meant to be a blessing.

Participants in the Study

Panel of Experts Who Nominated Participants

Name of panelist	Job title
Dr. Harlan Cleveland	Former ambassador to NATO; author of *Birth of a New World Order: An Open Moment for International Leadership*
Rev. Theodore Hesburgh	President Emeritus, University of Notre Dame
Mr. Frank Kelly	Former speech writer for President Harry Truman; Vice President, Nuclear Age Peace Foundation
Dr. Clark Kerr	President Emeritus, University of California
Mr. Jack Lowe	CEO of TD Industries, Dallas, TX; Vice President, Greenleaf Center, Indianapolis, IN
Dr. Oyar Oyen	Former rector, University of Bergen, Bergen, Norway
Dr. Kathleen Ross	President, Heritage College, Toppenish, WA

Ms. Kathy Ryan   Organizational consultant; author of
                                  Driving Fear Out of the Workplace

Ms. Margarita Mendoza   Senior Policy Coordinator for Affirma-
de Sugiyama   tive Action and EEOC, OFM,
                                  Governor's Office, State of Washington

List of Participants

Name of panelist	Job title
Donna Anderson	President, National Retiree Volunteer Coalition, Minneapolis, MN
Ron Anderson	President and CEO, Dallas County Hospital District, Dallas, TX
Sharon Anderson	Director, Reflective Leadership Center, University of Minnesota, Minneapolis, MN
Jane Dailey	Vice President—Nursing, South Fulton Medical Center, East Point, GA
William C. Friday	Executive Director, William R. Kenan, Jr., Charitable Trust, Chapel Hill, NC
Kathy Friedt	Director, Dept. of Licensing, Olympia, WA
Don George	Director, La Casa de Maria Retreat Center, Santa Barbara, CA
David Gershon	Director, Global Action Plan, Woodstock, NY

Theodore Hesburgh	President Emeritus, University of Notre Dame, Notre Dame, IN
Kerney Laday	Vice President—Field Operations, Xerox Corporation, Irving TX
Michael Lerner	Executive Director, COMMONWEAL, Bolinas, CA
Gene Liddell	Director, Department of Community Development, Olympia, WA
Roger Meier	COB Rodger Meier Cadillac, Dallas, TX
Jeannie O'Laughlin	President, Barry University, Miami Shores, FL
Claiborne Pell	United States Senator, Rhode Island
Bill Schoenhard	COO, SSM Health Care Systems, St. Louis, MO
Kent Skipper	Executive Director Salesmanship Club, Youth and Family Centers, Inc., Irving, TX
Bill Soloman	Chairman, President, CEO, Austin Industries, Dallas, TX
Marian Svinth	Employee Development Manager, Simpson Investment Company, Seattle, WA
Barbara Wiedner	Founder/Director, Grandmothers for Peace International, Elk Grove, CA
Martha Yallup	Deputy Director, Human Services, Yakima Indian Nation, Toppenish, WA

The Seven Consensus Statements from the Study

Participants in the study described in the introduction to this volume were asked the seven questions that appear below. Participants also approved the accompanying consensus statements or responses.

1. Describe what part—if any—spiritual traditions have played in the formation of your values/beliefs/ethics.
Spiritual traditions or principles have played a fundamental role in the formation of our values/ethics/beliefs.

2. What activities inspire, encourage, or renew you?
We are inspired, encouraged, and renewed by a variety of activities. While each one of us has found particular ways, there are some common activities. These activities include relationships with friends and colleagues, doing volunteer work in the community, enjoying nature, worship experiences (if we identify with a particular tradition), time with family, personal spiritual practices, listening to music, reading, physical recreation, and witnessing people overcome adversity.

3. Describe any community in which you participate that provides you with support, renewal, and insight.
We receive support, renewal, and insight from many different sources, which include our own work environment, community service and volunteer work, family, personal support groups, worship services (if we affiliate with a particular tradition), ethnic group of origin, and friends.

4. What are your central values?
Our central values include compassion for people and the earth, honesty,

integrity, justice, love, the importance of respecting differences, work, self-discernment, responsibility, and perseverance.

5. What does spirituality mean to you?
Spirituality is a very difficult word to define. An adequate definition would include reference to a relationship with something beyond myself (known as "Creator," "God," "transcendent power," etc.) which is intangible but also real. It would recognize that spirituality is the source of one's values and meaning, a way of understanding the world, an awareness of my "inner self," and a means of integrating the various aspects of myself into a whole.

6. Describe how your spirituality/central values influence your leadership practices.
Our spirituality has a profound impact on our leadership practices. It is the foundation of everything we do. It is our central frame of reference for helping us see our role in our organization in particular and our life as a whole. It keeps us focused on the needs and value of other people. It is expressed better in action than words.

7. Some contemporary writers on leadership and organizational studies are calling for greater integration of spirituality into the workplace. What is your reaction to this?
Spirituality is the basis for much of people's ways of understanding and acting in the world. Therefore, many of us believe it would be highly beneficial for secular organizations to find ways to recognize, affirm, and integrate it into the workplace and public life. This would allow people to have a sense of meaning and purpose—a connection to a greater good—beyond their individual selves. Others among us are opposed to an overt introduction of spirituality in the workplace, but are in favor of supporting leaders, colleagues, etc., whose behavior is congruent with spiritual concepts. All of us agree that, if an organization attempts integration, great care needs to be taken; respect for diversity and a mutual understanding of differences would be essential.

NOTES

1. Gareth Morgan, *Images of Organization* (Beverly Hills, Calif.: Sage Publications, 1986), 31.

2. William E. Diehl, *The Monday Connection: A Spirituality of Competence, Affirmation, and Support in the Workplace* (San Francisco: HarperCollins, 1991), 12.

3. Ibid., 15.

4. Having said this, I nevertheless will use the words "faith" and "spirituality" interchangeably in this book. I do that partly for semantic variety but also because, in practice within a Christian community, the words can become somewhat synonymous.

5. Quoted in Matthew Fox, *Sheer Joy: Conversations with Thomas Aquinas* (San Francisco: HarperSanFrancisco, 1992), 138.

6. Donald A. Schön, *The Reflective Practitioner: How Professionals Think in Action* (New York: Basic Books, 1983), 49.

7. H. Richard Niebuhr, *Christ and Culture* (New York: Harper and Row, 1951), 190ff.

8. J. Randall Nichols, *Building the Word: The Dynamics of Communication and Preaching* (San Francisco: Harper and Row, 1980), 108ff.

9. Paul Ricouer, *Interpretation Theory: Discourse and the Surplus of Meaning* (Fort Worth: Texas Christian University Press, 1976), 45.

10. Andrew Stark, "What's the Matter with Business Ethics?" *Harvard Business Review* (May-June 1993), 38-48.

11. Daniel Golman, *Emotional Intelligence: Why It Can Matter More Than IQ* (New York: Bantam Books, 1995), ix.

12. Robert Greenleaf, "Spirituality as Leadership," *Studies in Formative Spirituality* 3, no. 1 (1982): 13.

13. Peter Senge, *The Fifth Discipline: The Art and Practice of the Learning Organization* (New York: Doubleday, 1990), 205ff.

14. Max DePree, *Leadership Is an Art* (New York: Doubleday, 1989), 24.

15. Senge, *The Fifth Discipline*, 233ff.

16. Peter B. Vaill, *Learning as a Way of Being: Strategies for Survival in a World of Permanent White Water* (San Francisco: Jossey-Bass, 1996), 187-188.

17. Parker Palmer, "Leading from Within: Out of the Shadow, into the Light," in Jay A. Conger and Associates, *Spirit at Work: Discovering the Spirituality in Leadership* (San Francisco: Jossey-Bass, 1994), 23.

BIBLIOGRAPHY

Bolles, Richard N. *What Color is Your Parachute?* Berkeley: Ten Speed Press, 1990.

Conger, Jay A. and Asssociates. *Spirit at Work: Discovering the Sprituality in Leadership.* San Francisco: Jossey-Bass, 1994.

Covey, Stephen R. *The Seven Habits of Highly Successful People.* New York: Simon and Schuster, 1989.

_____. *First Things First: To Live, to Learn, to Leave a Legacy.* New York: Simon and Schuster, 1994.

DePree, Max. *Leadership Is an Art .* New York: Doubleday, 1989.

Diehl, William E. *The Monday Connection: A Spirituality of Competence, Affirmation, and Support in the Workplace.* San Francisco: Harper, 1991.

Fisher, Roger and William Ury. *Getting to Yes: Negotiating Without Giving In.* New York: Penguin, 1981.

Friedman, Edwin H. *Generation to Generation: Family Process in Church and Synagogue.* New York: Guilford Press, 1985.

Greenleaf, Robert K. *Servant Leadership: A Journey into the Nature of Legitimate Power and Greatness.* New York: Paulist Press, 1977.

Mead, Loren. *The Once and Future Church: Reinventing the Congregation for a New Mission Frontier.* Washington, D.C.: The Alban Institute, 1991.

Morgan, Gareth. *Images of Organization.* Berkeley: Sage Publications, 1986.

Nichols, J. Randall, *Building the Word: The Dynamics of Communication and Preaching.* San Francisco: Harper and Row, 1980.

Niebuhr, H. Richard *Christ and Culture.* New York: Harper and Row, 1951.

Parson, George D., and Speed B. Leas. *Understanding Your Congregation as a System.* Washington, DC: The Alban Institute, 1993.

Reber, Robert E. *Linking Faith and Daily Life: An Educational Program for Lay People.* Washington, DC: The Alban Institute, 1991. (Out of print.)

Ricouer, Paul. *Interpretation Theory: Discourse and the Surplus of Meaning.* Fort Worth: Texas Christian University Press, 1976.

Schon, Donald. *The Reflective Practitioner: How Professionals Think in Action.* New York: Basic Books, 1983.

Senge, Peter M. *The Fifth Discipline: The Art and Practice of the Learning Organization.* New York: Doubleday, 1990.

Steinke, Peter L. *How Your Church Family Works: Understanding Congregations as Emotional Systems.* Washington, DC: The Alban Institute, 1993.

Vaill, Peter B. *Learning as a Way of Being: Strategies for Survival in a World of Permanent White Water.* San Francisco: Jossey-Bass, 1996.

The Alban Institute:
an invitation to membership

The Alban Institute, begun in 1974, believes that the congregation is essential to the task of equipping the people of God to minister in the church and the world. A multi-denominational membership organization, the Institute provides on-site training, educational programs, consulting, research, and publishing for hundreds of churches across the country.

The Alban Institute invites you to be a member of this partnership of laity, clergy, and executives—a partnership that brings together people who are raising important questions about congregational life and people who are trying new solutions, making new discoveries, finding a new way of getting clear about the task of ministry. The Institute exists to provide you with the kinds of information and resources you need to support your ministries.

Join us now and enjoy these benefits:

CONGREGATIONS: The Alban Journal, a highly respected journal published six times a year, to keep you up to date on current issues and trends.

Inside Information, Alban's quarterly newsletter, keeps you informed about research and other happenings around Alban. Available to members only.

Publications Discounts:

- ☐ 15% for Individual, Retired Clergy, and Seminarian Members
- ☐ 25% for Congregational Members
- ☐ 40% for Judicatory and Seminary Executive Members

Discounts on Training and Education Events

Write our Membership Department at the address below or call us at 1-800-486-1318 or 301-718-4407 for more information about how to join The Alban Institute's growing membership, particularly about Congregational Membership in which 12 designated persons receive all benefits of membership.

The Alban Institute, Inc.
Suite 433 North
4550 Montgomery Avenue
Bethesda, MD 20814-3341